AMERICAN GARDENS

A Tour of the Nation's Finest Private Gardens

PETER LOEWER

Produced by The Philip Lief Group

Simon and Schuster

New York   London   Toronto   Sydney   Tokyo

Published by Simon and Schuster
A Division of Simon & Schuster Inc.
Simon & Schuster Building
Rockefeller Center
1230 Avenue of the Americas
New York, New York 10020

SIMON AND SCHUSTER and colophon are registered trademarks of
Simon & Schuster Inc.

Library of Congress Cataloging in Publication Data
Loewer, H. Peter.
    American gardens.
    "Produced by the Philip Lief Group, Inc."
    Includes index.
    1. Gardens—United States.   2. Gardens—United
States—Design.   3. Gardens—United States—Pictorial
works.   4. United States—Description and travel—
1981–   . I. Philip Lief Group.   II. Title.
SB466.U6L62   1988   712'.6'0973   88-3252
ISBN 0-671-66267-8

Pennsylvania Rock Garden was adapted from an article that first appeared in the
October, 1983 issue of *American Horticulturist*

Photographs in A Tennessee Garden appear courtesy of *Southern Living* Magazine

Quotes from "The Plantsman's Garden," Lester Hawkins, *Pacific Horticulture*,
Spring 1984, used with the permission of W. George Waters.

A portion of "Mending Wall" by Robert Frost reprinted with the permission of
Henry Holt and Co.

A portion of "This is the Garden" by E.E. Cummings reprinted with the permission
of W.W. Norton and Company, Inc.

A portion of "Chicago" by Carl Sandburg reprinted with the permission of
Harcourt Brace Johanovich, Inc.

A portion of "One Perfect Rose" by Dorothy Parker reprinted with the permission
of Viking Penguin.

Photography by Judith Bromley, Ken Druse, Alan Eliel, Derek Fell, Felice Frankel,
Robert Frasier, Pamela J. Harper, Margaret A. Hensel, Bruce Krasberg, Peter
Loewer, Beth Maynor, Elvin McDonald, Gary Mottau, John Neubauer, John Occelli,
Doan Ogden, Joanne and Jerry Pavia, Kathlene Persoff, Judith Phillips, Larry
Rhodes, Allan R. Taylor, Tom Tynan, and Volkmar K. Wentzel.

Book design and composition by The Sarabande Press
Manufactured in the United States of America
10   9   8   7   6   5   4   3   2   1

CONTENTS

PART TWO

Great Ideas for Your Garden

PREFACE

Over the past year I have talked to many American gardeners about their gardens. In most cases I have interrupted these intrepid men and women in their duties, for when I needed their help they were usually planting, often planning, sometimes weeding, but always working. In every case they dropped trowel or plant, pot or hoe, and instantly became veritable fountains of information. They told me stories about the joys and hardships of gardening, they entertained me with their successes and sorrowed me with their defeats, and they always had time to ask questions about my own gardening experiences. In the end I have learned a great deal about this country and its gardens. Without their help and assistance, this book would not have been possible.

The same holds true for the photographers. They, too, deserve praise for their fine pictures of these gardens and the plants they contain.

There is one more person, without whom the book would never have seen the light of the gardening day. That person is Anne Halpin, who not only had the original idea for doing a book on American gardens, but who has also acted as both the editor and the general factotum—the second job, by the way, represents a position that nobody wants but every book project of this size must have.

And once again there is a great deal of help to acknowledge from friends: my wife Jean, who is always there; Budd Myers for his excellent research; David and Joan Pitkin for the California connection; Frank and Marge Martin for the North Carolina connection; Art Kozelka of Chicago; and Lisa Govan and Joe Freedman for the beautiful design of this book.

Peter Loewer,
Cochecton, 1988.

INTRODUCTION

*How deeply seated in the human heart is
the liking for gardens and gardening.*
ALEXANDER SMITH (1830-1867)

Fast food and fast times: the summing up of the middle American lifestyle, if you believe everything you read or the commercials you see on television. When gardening is added to the equation, that same lifestyle is pictured as though it's played out against a background of closely clipped and chemically green lawns bordered about the edges with yellow clots of marigolds and wavy-edged petunias drooping in the summer heat. Black macadam driveways resembling old-fashioned licorice strips are lined on either side with lollipopped evergreens that connect gray roadways to one-, two-, or three-car garages.

The misconceptions do not stop with suburbia. When you see what most people think of as the homes and gardens of successful people belonging to the *monde*, the landscape is viewed as being just as unimaginative as those surrounding tract houses, merely more expensive. To see such views confirmed, one need only glance at the display of properties sold through the back pages of

The New Yorker or *The New York Times Magazine*, or the other newsstand publications devoted entirely to selling expensive homes and estates, where old or new homes of stone with colonial peaks and slate roofs are landscaped with the obligatory mugo pines, and the most blatant of the puce rhododendrons in company with the fierce flame of the orange azalea.

And consider the popularly presented view of the American avant-garde at play in the garden, the type found in the slickest of the decorating magazines. In these fashionable settings, cunning people have peppered the land with sculpture too large for even the gardens at Versailles: lush photo spreads show us life-size cutouts of pine trees (striped with confetti colors), or tree limbs bound with dyed ribbons of plastic in a sort of miniature attempt at imitating what Christo could do if he wrapped the gardens at Kew.

Back at the other end of the garden spectrum are more stereotypes. Consider the organic gardener, a person who is often imagined to be dedicated only to the preservation of giant redwoods and dolphins. The organic gardener, to many people, is someone who shuns all things chemical but will lay strips of black plastic between rows of vegetables as a mulch against weeds; who grows only those flowers known to cause problems for noxious insects, and who cultivates these blossoms merely as a colorful backdrop to tomatoes as big as bowling balls.

As if these misunderstandings about gardening in America were not bad enough, we must also endure the pronouncements of the garden pundits who continually pressure us to garden as the English do. We are constantly told that the only gardens worth emulating resemble those found at Tresco Abbey in the Isles of Scilly, Christopher Lloyd's mixed border at Great Dixter, or one-color gardens like the all-white garden at Sissinghurst*.

Now, I would be the first to admit that the above-mentioned gardens are quite beautiful. Would that I *could* pattern my garden after Great Dixter or Tresco Abbey and grow *Mahonia* 'Lionel Fortescue'; enjoy a *succes fou* with a wall covered by tree lupines (*Lupinus arboreus*); or fly by helicopter from Penzance to the Isles of Scilly and bring back yellow mimosa (*Acacia baileyana*) to bloom in my garden at Christmas.

Unfortunately when dealing with English gardens, the one constant that everyone neglects to mention is the path of the Gulf Stream, an oceanic river that bathes those sceptred isles with warm water so that temperatures below zero are unheard of and

ever-mild winters alternate the seasons with early springs, late falls, and cool and damp summers. This situation is found in America only along the northern Pacific coast.

These same advisors also forget that England enjoyed a period of centuries when the ships of the empire sailed around the world to bring back plants both rare and unusual for the gardens of the royalty, the privileged, and the rising middle class. Here in America, the country was engaged in the foundation of a democracy and had little time for such niceties. There are only a few three-hundred-year-old lawns in the United States.

No, the art of gardening in America is an altogether different story. On a typical day in early January in a country some thirty-eight times larger than Great Britain and Ireland combined, the North Central states will have temperatures touching 0°F and will be buried under 3 feet of snow, while it will be raining and a balmy 60°F in Los Angeles, sleeting over Manhattan, and people will be swimming and golfing in Miami Beach.

How can there be one kind of garden in a country of such climatic diversity? The answer is, of course, there can't.

Before the inception of the interstate highway system in the United States you could drive across America from city to city and town to town and pass gardens as individual as the area in which they began.

You saw bungalows with pecan trees and honeysuckle; white farm houses with lilacs in the front yard and later in the season, rows of blooming hollyhocks along the side of the garage; vegetable gardens so lush they had an elegance all their own. Daylilies and roses bloomed, rose-of-Sharon and delphiniums bloomed, globe flowers and sweet Williams bloomed, and cactus and sagebrush turned the deserts to wonderlands every spring. But with the passing of the Route 66s from the map of America, most of us are forced to drive the fast lanes and believe that the world

*There is an irony in that last preference. Vita Sackville-West worked with an all-white garden in 1939 and is widely thought to have originated the idea. But the original plan probably came from an American. The Honorable Ben. Perley Poore designed such a garden at Newburyport, Massachusetts in 1833, calling it his moonlight garden.

of the individual American garden has vanished forever.

It hasn't.

Television leads us to think that everything from New Jersey to Arizona looks like a manicured suburbia with a patch of lawn, a barbecue pit, and a line of Pfitzer junipers along the sidewalk.

It doesn't.

The gardens that are featured in this book all prove the point that gardening in America is as diverse as its culture and doing quite well. In fact, the total retail sales for American lawn and garden care in 1986 totaled an all-time high of 17.49 billion dollars.

All the gardens in this book, except one, are privately owned. They vary in size from less than an acre up to twelve acres. Some are on square lots; others on surveyor's nightmares. Some of the owners had professional help in the overall design of their garden; others did everything on their own. Some owners have outside help with regular garden chores; others do everything themselves. The gardens are located in New England, the North, the South, the Midwest, and the Far West and each one is individual and endemic to the area in which it is found. Whether perched on the side of a mountain in northeastern Pennsylvania, set in the deserts of southern California, or sprouting from the rooftops of Manhattan, these are personal and private gardens, worked on and cared for by individual men and women, and all truly American in both their design and their philosophy.

But in a book like this it really isn't enough to regale the senses with page after page of glorious color pictures without giving you the views of the gardeners concerned. In the various interviews, I have tried to do just that and, at the same time, give you some idea of just how old, in years, America is.

In Part Two of the book, there are thirty-six pages of ideas, some of them from gardens profiled in Part One and some from other sources. They vary from the use of sculpture in the garden to a number of very unusual plants that are available from one or more of the sources listed in the Appendix. These illustrations are for you to consider, and perhaps adapt, for use in your own garden, whether it lies in New Mexico or New Hampshire.

But whatever your garden will be, remember the lines of Goethe:

Knowst thou the land where the lemon
trees bloom,
Where the gold orange glows in the deep
thicket's gloom,
Where a wind ever soft from the blue
heaven blows,
And the groves are of laurel and myrtle
and rose?

I know. Of course, it's America.

PART ONE

The Gardens

A GARDEN ON A ROCK

A FOURTEENTH CENTURY JAPANESE poet named Kenko once wrote:

"Too much furniture in one's living room. . .

Too many rocks, trees, and herbs in a garden. . ."

If he saw the garden of Margot Parrot, however, he would have to retract the second line, for this is a garden built upon a wonderful collection of rocks.

The Parrot garden is located in the town of Manchester, Massachusetts, on the rockbound Atlantic coast between the cities of Salem and Gloucester.

Although the Parrot property is just under three acres, it boasts a lawn, a small orchard, some beautiful trees, a wall of tufa—that wondrous and porous rock rich in lime and loved by rock garden plants—and a very old house built sometime in the late 1600s. But it is the flower-bedecked rock that immediately commands all your attention. The lichen-spattered boulders that sit balanced on the master rock are home to hundreds of alpine plants, *Androsace* to *Iris* and *Daphne* to *Rhododendron*, and even when not in flower their leaves grace the granite surface with sparkling greens and grays.

The first thing I asked was the date the garden began.

"I would say it started in a small way around 1962," said Mrs. Parrot. "We did all the work ourselves. My husband helped with the heavy hauling and lifting and I did the

---

Left, part of the cliff, with several varieties of *Phlox subulata, Aurinia saxatilis, Schivereckia podolica, Draba* spp., *Arabis* spp., *Aquilegia canadensis,* and dwarf conifers. *Above, Dicentra eximia,* the fringed bleeding heart.

Mrs. Parrot on top of the cliff.

choosing of the plant material, but it was a cooperative effort.

"We lived here about ten years before we paid any attention to the rock. After all, it was completely covered with wild grape and honeysuckle vines and literally overgrown. But right next to the sun porch there is a low outcrop of rock, a kind of shelf, where another owner had at one time planted some maiden pinks (*Dianthus deltoides*), and every spring a few flowers would appear.

"I couldn't resist and began to pull back the grasses to give the struggling plant a chance. It was difficult to garden because we had little children at the time and a great deal of work to do on the house. But I would look around and see little places for a bit of soil. I planted some rock cresses (*Arabis* spp.) and they did so well that I began to get interested in this type of gardening.

"Each year we cleared away more of the grapevines and the honeysuckle. If we had known when we moved in what the garden would eventually become, there would have been more planning."

The wonderful thing about having a rock garden is the number of plants that can be pushed comfortably into a small space as compared with a perennial border or island bed. Using the resources of the American Rock Garden Society's seed exchange, the Parrots began to propagate and expand their collection.

"I was always bored with the idea of weeding 20-some feet of border, but gardening on the rock was different. Then I thought there must be more than just putting one plant in a spot of dirt so I joined the American Rock Garden Society (ARGS), started to read their wonderful *Bulletin*, began visiting other gardens, and used the seed listings to start new plants.

"But," she continued, "as the years went by, the seeds got ahead of me. There were just too many of them and my heart was bigger than my head when it came to choosing. In the end I just stayed with the ARGS seed exchange."

Mrs. Parrot noticed vertical cracks in the rock, open slits that had originally been covered by the vines and now contained a heavy, black, rotted humus that was very tightly packed.

"At the beginning," she said, "I picked them clean and refilled the openings with a mix containing all the prescribed and proper ingredients, but I never could manage to make it as dense as the material I was replacing. I finally decided to leave well enough alone and used what was there. When I tucked seeds in those cracks in early spring, they would germinate beautifully."

The Parrots have no greenhouse, but they do keep a cold frame measuring about 4 by 9 feet and also maintain a misting system for propagation.

When asked how many plants are in the garden, Mrs. Parrot thought for a moment then said:

"I started a list and arrived at a total of about seven hundred fifty by counting the plants per quarter inch."

Even with the Atlantic Ocean close by, the Parrot garden is in USDA hardiness Zone 5, complicated with the typical Northeast climate in which winters can be without snow-cover and summers without rain for days and weeks on end. The Parrots quickly learned about water problems and buried flexible

Top, a pool in the face of the cliff. *Bottom,* a balanced boulder with yellow *Aurinia saxatilis* 'Citrina', white *Schivereckia podolica,* and red *Aquilegia canadensis.*

hose with sprinkler heads about the garden, for, by the end of a typical summer's day, the rock could become very warm, if not hot.

For a time the Parrots worked hard at winter protection but they soon found that the less they did, the better were the results the following spring. They finally covered only two or three favorite plants. Luckily they have no deer problem; the pest population is limited to chipmunks, mice, rabbits, and of course, slugs.

I asked Mrs. Parrot which were her favorite plants.

"My word!" she exclaimed, "What an order! It's very difficult to narrow it down to much below the original seven hundred. But if you really want a few, I love *Arenaria montana* because it is so very white and makes such lovely mats. And *Penstemon rupicola* for its gorgeous cherry red and the fact that it loves to grow in narrow cracks on the cliff. Then there is *Phyteuma comosum,* a strange little flower that grows in the tufa cliff (and is also a favorite of the slugs). And *Glaucidium palmatum,* a wonderful woodland plant from Japan, and the spectacular blue *Lithospermum diffusum* 'Heavenly Blue'. But this leaves out all the wonderful phloxes and columbines and drabas, and the daphne, and that charming *Linaria* hybrid. . ."

MAKING THE GRADE

HOLLISTON, MASSACHUSETTS, IS A town some twenty miles southwest of Boston that was settled about 1659 (that's ten years before the death of Rembrandt). Because of its proximity to what is affectionately known as Bean Town, land that was once best left alone is now being developed into lots with new homes plunked squarely in the middle.

Most people who have purchased such homes know about the problem of fill. The original land that supports the house must be elevated from the surrounding area that is usually too rocky or too wet for construction. Rather than rework the land entirely, the builders import vast amounts of dirt—not always of the best quality—to raise the grade. New homeowners are then faced with a house surrounded by a rectangle of barren earth that

soon reminds them of being all alone, locked inside a car without a key, in the middle of an empty suburban shopping mall at high noon.

When the then-owners of this garden bought their newly built home, at least they knew that the three-quarters of an acre of created desert around them was historic dirt if nothing else. And because the contractor thought he might himself move into the house, the soil used for fill was better than average and included a lot of sand.

The first problem was, of course, the site. The area around the house had been built up for a septic system and a landscape architect had designed a formal planting for around the house, so a bluestone walk was put into place and some additional topsoil brought in. A little patio was constructed on the south side of the house.

Left, conifers and rhododendrons are planted near the deck. *Kalmia latifolia* and *Euonymus fortunei* 'Emerald 'n Gold' flank the boulders at center. In the foreground are, from left, dwarf purple barberry, *Pinus mugo* var. *mugo*, *Juniperus procumbens* var. *nana*, and *Ilex crenata* var. *convexa*. *Above,* rock cress.

"They called me," said Gary Mottau, the garden's designer, "to create a garden with year-round interest. They wanted a profusion of color and a great diversity of plant material as quickly as possible, anything to fill in the now-open space. To make matters worse, the bare areas were in the middle of a wooded two acres so perfection was within view but completely out of reach."

Mr. Mottau has been gardening since his preschool years and he did yard work all through secondary school. While in college he ran a landscape maintenance business, and after receiving a master's degree in landscape architecture he worked for a time with Jim Crockett, before going into business for himself in 1977.

Immediately, Mr. Mottau thought of a number of distinct theme areas for the garden in Holliston, knowing that while some took time to develop others would give satisfaction quickly. He planned a spot with dwarf conifers, a wild-type area close to the edge of the woods, a rock garden on part of the slope, a deck and a patio, and a grassed enclave with a small pool. Each area would have a distinct microclimate: one wet, one dry, and one shady. Screen plantings would eventually hide the house from the street.

"We brought in 150 cubic yards of topsoil," said Mr. Mottau, "and one hundred bales of peat moss, and I did my own composting off the site to add to the total. I brought in some 50 cubic yards of horse manure, and because the topsoil was heavy, added some 20 cubic yards of coarse sand and even contracted to haul out some peat from a logging site nearby.

"For the rock garden I found a stone worker, William Brady, who was also responsible for planting the 10- to 12-inch caliper white pines. We also brought in wild moss (that would eventually spread to more favorable spots) and woodland ferns from other building sites after getting the owners'

A rock garden with a rich carpet of greens, contains rhododendron, yew, two cultivars of *Euonymus fortunei*, dwarf mugo pine, and yellow-green lemon thyme.

A "river" of *Lamium maculatum* 'Beacon Silver' flows over a ledge of rocks to merge with Waukegan junipers and *Euonymus fortunei* 'Emerald Gaiety'.

permission. And, be warned: Use one source for rocks so the color matches. It's the same problem as matching wallpaper. It's also important to remember that ground-hugging junipers and other ground covering plants are much better under the shrubbery than the yearly toil of replacing bare bark chips."

The first phase was to plant a basic evergreen structure around the house using good-sized container trees. They immediately put in a 6-inch caliper scarlet oak (*Quercus coccinea*), even though the job began in November. Next came a *Chamaecyparis obtusa* 'Gracilis Aurea' whose bright yellow leaves would serve as a beacon on the hilltop. Dwarf Alberta spruce (*Picea glauca* 'Conica') were put about 40 feet from the kitchen window; they would eventually grow together and provide year-round color. Then beyond, about 150 feet away from the house and to ultimately screen out the road, they planted 3-inch caliper white pines (*Pinus strobus*), about 8 to 10 feet apart, in groupings with dogwoods in front so the blossoms would show up against a background of needles. Bigger specimens of the dwarf or slow-growing plants were used but the plan was to keep them in scale over the next five to ten years.

On the north side of the house Mr. Mottau used blue holly (*Ilex × Meservaeae* 'Blue Princess'), the thread-leaved *Chamaecyparis pisifera* 'Filifera', a little concrete retaining wall covered up with *Forsythia × intermedia*, and some Waukegan junipers (*Juniperus horizontalis* 'Douglasii'), the last for their fine winter coloring of rich purple-blue.

"The garden as pictured," he said, "is about two and one-half years old. I think that it looks much older than that. To get this effect in a new garden, the owner should try and use plenty of dwarf conifers. If you cannot afford to buy the larger sizes, choose the smaller plants and be patient. But try to buy a few large specimen plants to give a feeling of permanence to the site. Be careful what you plant around the house; try for prunable material that can be cut back if windows start to be covered. Use groundcovers like myrtle (*Vinca minor*) because they cut down on maintenance. With proper light conditions and good soil the plants are going to grow, and in two to three years the rewards are well worth the investment in both time and money — that is," he smiled, "if you like gardening."

COLORS IN AN
AMERICAN GARDEN

IN THE SECOND HALF of the eighteenth century, it was popular to have an American-type garden in England. A London merchant, Peter Collinson, arranged with John Bartram of Philadelphia to send over seeds which were then distributed to various landscape architects, and American gardens were designed for many of the great homes of England. But soon—ironically—new species arrived from all over the world and eventually outnumbered and crowded out the American plants. By the end of the First World War, the term "American garden" died a natural death, although at least one garden survives at Fonthill Abbey in Wiltshire.

Elsa Bakalar is a teacher of English who

became an English transplant. She arrived in this country some forty years ago. She worked in the British Foreign Service in New York City for ten years and with her husband began to come up to the country on weekends—not for a ritzy thing to do but because those two days out of Manhattan are often necessary to the survival of the mind. The Bakalars weekended from 1956 to 1977, then late in that year left the city to live in a summer house in northwestern Massachusetts.

The land is on top of a hill (some 1,800 feet in elevation) near the small town of Heath. Heath, in turn, is some twenty miles from Deerfield and not too far from Brattleboro, Vermont, in an area of the country that was originally settled before 1670 (that was four

*Left, **Delphinium** hybrids in shades of blue-violet, purple, and white are surrounded by white phlox, deep purple lavender, red dahlias, rich yellow golden marguerites, rosy pink sidalcea, and soft yellow daylilies. **Above**, a grandiflora rose, 'Queen Elizabeth', with Asiatic hybrid lilies 'Sterling Star' (white) and 'Chinook'.*

years after the great Fire of London destroyed St. Paul's cathedral). It's still a part of the country where telephones have a double ring, a sound that's warm and friendly in a world that reveres the trilling of the contemporary electronic phone system.

When they first arrived in the country, Mrs. Bakalar remembered her English childhood and pictures flashed through her mind of the great English gardens. She decided to have such a garden to work in on weekends. "But it didn't work," she said. "The climate is just too different. After all, the Thames River rarely freezes but here we have been known to plunge to -20°F."

This is Zone 5 country with isolated pockets of Zone 4. In midwinter, -10°F is normal and on many occasions the wind is a continual enemy.

When asked how she became so interested in gardening, Mrs. Bakalar said, "Like many children in gardening families, I was hauled—kicking—into the garden as a child and told to weed. The result of such treatment is a violent dislike for anything to do with gardening, that is, until I had a place of my own with a little plot of earth. Then it's funny how the love of gardening seeps into your soul even before you're aware of it and you find yourself, once again, down on hands and knees in the dirt."

And how does she care for the garden? "I am now a fulltime gardener," she continued. "During the best part of the year I'm out here almost forty hours a week. However I do get some help from my husband. And I also get help from books because I read everything I can get my hands on." She adds with a smile in her voice, "That is, during the winter only."

Mrs. Bakalar has been teaching classes in gardening for about five years. After working at the local community college she wanted to get out of the office and began to initiate off-campus garden workshops. "Now I keep my own garden plus nine others. But my advice to those who wish to garden has always been: if I can do it you can do it. So I show them how.

"And I have advice for the housewife who wants to garden. I have arthritis in my hand so it hurts when I dust but not when I'm out potting and digging about. If I have any counsel to potential gardeners, especially women, it's to stop dusting. It's the first thing that should go when time is short."

Her garden is actually a patchwork of individual gardens, pieces here and there that add up to about an acre on a property of about five acres that includes a pond, a big meadow, and some woods.

I asked Mrs. Bakalar for a list of her favorite flowers.

"I have a finicky and sentimental attachment for delphiniums," she answered. "I belong to the Delphinium Society and of course use their seed exchange. Did you know there are over three hundred named varieties? Of course, summer storms are a terrible problem hereabouts, especially with tall bloomers like delphiniums. I've been known to rush out in a wind and use cellophane tape to hold a flower up. In one eighteen-hour course that I teach, I spend two to three hours telling people how to hold flowers up without using those awful bamboo stakes. I've seen some gardens where there are more stakes and twine than regular flowers."

She favors the system called pea staking, an English practice that involves placing twigs and branches pruned from trees upright in a perennial bed early in the season. The plants grow up through the openings in the sticks and eventually cover them with foliage. The name comes from the vegetable garden, where the method was used to hold up pea vines.

Getting back to delphiniums she continued, "There is one yellow delphinium that the seed catalogs call 'Zalil'. It's really *Delphinium semibarbatum*. The problem with it is it can go dormant and most people think that it's dead. You have to mark the seedlings carefully in the nursery bed

so when they disappear they will be noticed. I grow big clumps of it. It has a long wiry stem and looks a bit raggedy so I crowd it below with other flowers including *Delphinium* 'Connecticut Yankee'. But the color is superb. And it makes the most beautiful dried flower."

"I like lilies quite well," she added, "but not excessively. I love billowing masses of flowers. And the gray leaves of lavender and the texture of bugloss or *Anchusa*. Poppies are wonderful flowers, though many American gardeners seem to have a bit of a problem with the opium poppy, not realizing that it's quite possible to grow it for the beautiful flowers without getting involved in any of the darker side of its use or history."

Like many a master gardener Mrs. Bakalar has some definite ideas on color. "Well," she said, "I've always been bothered by people who call a flower 'plain yellow' or who say 'that's just red' or 'that's blue.' I like to be precise about colors. After all, there's a world of difference between rust red and scarlet, and lemon yellow and golden yellow. There are warm yellows and cold yellows, light or dark yellows, and a world of blues. After all, blues go with practically anything, especially with soft yellows.

"And I'm fond of various combinations of color. I've had astonishing luck mixing rose with red and highlighting with a little orange. The result is quite delightful. It reminds me of the

brightness found in that Indian cloth where little pieces of mirror are added. I wouldn't wear the fabric in Massachusetts but the colors are beautiful in the garden."

In one section of her garden Mrs. Bakalar mixes the golden yellow of *Ligularia stenocephala* 'The Rocket', the blue of *Delphinium chinensis* 'Blue Mirror', the lilac blue of *Campanula carpatica*, steel blue globe thistles (*Echinops sphaerocephalus*), and 'Connecticut Lemonglow' lilies. It's not a hodgepodge but a coordinated rhythm of color with just the right amount of red provided by *Phlox* 'Leo Schlacter' and highlights with the white 'Miss Lingard.' The background for this composition is the woodlands of the property.

"A background for a garden is another problem here in the States," Mrs. Bakalar said. "After all we're not overly endowed with three hundred-year-old yew hedges and marvelous old brick and stone walls left over from ancient monasteries or sacked ancestral seats. Yet many of these gardens need something other than blue sky to play against.

A section of the main perennial garden, east of the house, looking downhill. The color scheme blends soft yellows with purples and many shades of blue. White is added for a lift; gray and silver-leaved plants and a few crimson reds add interest.

"There is a view looking out to New Hampshire from the side of our hill with that tremendous bowl of blue overhead.

"You can get a wonderful view of the garden or take great photos by getting down on your stomach, but who really wants to look at the garden from that viewpoint or ask guests to do so? Flower beds look best when they are viewed against some kind of backdrop. Luckily we have a woods—a second-growth pasture with a mix of saplings but luckily containing some white birch—that runs down the south side of the hill, far enough away from the beds that it doesn't cause a shade problem. And the pond also makes a marvelous foil for the flowers."

When she planned those beds she would walk up and down the hill to check to see how the planting combinations would look, then run back up and plan again.

Mrs. Bakalar has some favorite American plants, especially those from the Midwest:

"Part of it revolves around being romantic and probably unrealistic about the prairies. Most likely the feeling comes from reading those books by Willa Cather. I may be kidding myself, maybe they don't populate what's left of the prairies with those marvelous flowers, but blazing stars (*Liatris* spp.), the beautiful purple coneflower (*Echi-*

Mrs. Bakalar stakes tall hybrid delphiniums. *Lavandula angustifolia* 'Hidcote' blooms in the foreground. Behind it are *Anthemis tinctoria, Phlox carolina* 'Miss Lingard', *Lilium* 'Connecticut Lemonglow', and *Hemerocallis* 'Hyperion'.

nacea purpurea), and the charming black-eyed Susan (*Rudbeckia hirta*) smack of the prairie. And they have a roughness and sturdiness that to me makes them wonderful when put together with softer and gentler flowers. Obviously they look like no–nonsense blossoms that had to be tough to survive the winds and weather on the prairies. Then there is the New England aster, a plant that went to England and came back to America but this time more expensive (as a result of breeding).

"And what can I say about the California poppy (*Eschscholtzia californica*)? One year I actually went out and cut down blooming delphiniums and other ornamental poppies because the colors fought with the bright gold of the Californians. I felt it was impossible to look at."

And just to make sure she doesn't run out of things to do, Mrs. Bakalar is about to begin writing a book about her garden and her ideas about gardening.

So the gardens of Elsa Bakalar will continue to grow. Right now she's increasingly interested in the ornamental grasses. Not only are they a welcome addition to the perennial bed, they turn beautiful shades of russet and golden brown in the winter and look so beautiful against the background of a New England snow.

A BOTANIC GARDEN
IN THE BERKSHIRES

Two MILES WEST OF Stockbridge, Massachusetts, on Route 102 lies the Berkshire Garden Center. It is the only public garden in this book. It was created to both serve and instruct the public and remains to this day an important center of garden activity in the area.

Founded in 1934, it illustrates a very American approach to gardening. Walter Prichard Eaton wrote the following in a garden center publication of 1954: ". . . in one of the corners of a cross-roads in Stockbridge, a garden appeared. It was unlike any other garden in the Berkshires because it stood open for everybody to visit. In fact, its purpose was to entice everybody to visit—to see what lilies were most attractive, what roses are hardiest, what annuals, especially among the new varieties, are most desirable.

"The Garden Center is a teacher by the wayside, telling all who pass what beauty and what happiness can be achieved by putting seeds in the ground. How many old gardens it has improved, how many new gardens it has inspired, who can say?"

Six garden clubs and seven organizations founded the center. Beginning with an initial donation of estate property, the center became a gathering place where amateur gardeners could meet with others of like minds. A reference library was started, a file of seed and plant catalogs maintained, and the services of a resident horticulturist would eventually carry on an experimental garden, give advice and information free to all members, and open a plant

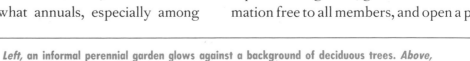

Left, an informal perennial garden glows against a background of deciduous trees. *Above,* *Primula* × *polyantha* hybrids bloom in late April and May.

and seed exchange. It became a true botanic garden.

The original property was on the south side of the road and the rest of the acreage was picked up in bits and pieces. They bought the final piece of woods in the late 1960s. Today there are fourteen acres with about eight in woodland.

The present horticulturist is David Burdick.

"This is one of the few public gardens," said Mr. Burdick, "that really invite you to interact with the plants—to touch and smell them as you walk through. Anything that we do, you can reproduce at home. That is what our displays try to say. We don't intimidate potential plant lovers with pristine neatness, something that is very hard for most homeowners to accomplish. Our philosophy is probably best expressed in a remark made by a now retired worker, who always left a small spot in his assigned areas unweeded, explaining that, 'We don't want the place looking like the Ritz!'"

There are many theme gardens in the Center. The Idea Garden is raised to a convenient height for people who may have trouble bending or who use a wheelchair. Many rock garden plants, scented plants, herbs and vegetables, and small perennials are used to demonstrate the wide range of plants that can grow in a small area.

The Procter Garden features salt-tolerant shrubs—a fence installed to keep

Forget-me-nots, foamflower, lily-of-the-valley, and ferns grow among rocks.

road salt from splashing plants is not perfect and salt still seeps into the soil—and includes rock garden plants, roses, foxgloves, and delphiniums, all in soft pastel shades.

The Herb Garden includes low stone walls and stepping stones to keep visitors' shoes dry when they are out picking herbs. There are many beds of medicinal and culinary herbs, herbs with interesting histories. Visitors are invited to rub the leaves together to sample herb aromas.

The Rose Garden is planted with species that are hardy to the Berkshires. In order to enjoy a full season of bloom, annual and perennial flowers are planted among the roses.

The day I talked to Mr. Burdick, the center was busy with demonstrations of maple sugaring to a large group of local school children.

"The maple sugaring," he said, "is the first event of the year for the children. And children are important to us."

"And Stockbridge," said Mr. Burdick, "was the home of Norman Rockwell for the last twenty years or so of his life. There is a museum of his work nearby and the town thrives on tourism because of it. Rockwell often pedalled his bike down to the BGC to sketch in the rose garden or just quietly sit and enjoy the solitude of the pond."

I think that knowing about Rockwell makes the Berkshire Garden Center one of the most American gardens of all.

WALLED PERENNIAL GARDEN

NORTH EGREMONT, MASSACHUSETTS, is about six miles northwest of South Egremont and less than a quarter of a mile from the New York State border. The town was founded in 1775. North Egremont had previously been part of Little York and in 1731 was purchased from the Indians for thirty pounds and a suit of clothes.

Mr. Edward R. Bulkeley is the present owner of about three acres of property in North Egremont that were originally part of a larger farm. Back in the 1930s, the land became a private home and included an extensive garden, designed and planted to emulate the contemporary notion of an English walled garden. The garden covers about a quarter of an acre, and consists of a series of walls made of native stone plus walkways and terraces, some so settled that they look far older than their years.

The concept of walled gardens reaches far back in history. There is a plan for one such garden described in Albert Forbes Sieveking's book, *Gardens Ancient and Modern* (1899). This garden belonged to a prosperous Egyptian of Thebes and was so beloved by him that he wished to take it along into the next world.

"When we bought the house back in 1972," said Mr. Bulkeley, "it was rather forlorn looking and best described as a formal English garden with lots of evergreens, yews, and euonymus. We removed much of what was here and brought in many perennials."

The perennials, of course, have brought a

Left, the rock garden in early spring before the paper birch (*Betula papyrifera*) has leafed out. *Above,* oriental poppies (*Papaver orientale*) and other late spring perennials.

marvelous wash of color to the gardens. But one of the first flowers to catch the eye is a clump of the annual white spider flower (*Cleome Hasslerana* 'Helen Campbell'), sparkling brighter than the roses and alyssum that line one walkway, creating a scene that is out of the ordinary. An old white-painted bench shines even brighter than the cleome. "It was here when we arrived," said Mr. Bulkeley, "and has graced the area for all these years."

"I work on the roses and the vegetables," he added, "but if you really want to know about the flowers you must talk to my horticulturist, Barbara Bockbrader."

I talked to Ms. Bockbrader about the plants and the plantings before she had to dash off to a meeting. She has been working with Mr. Bulkeley for the past ten years and in addition to a busy life as a horticulturist, she sits on the town's local conservation commission.

"This is really a June garden," she said. "and the roses are quite beautiful. We have 'Queen Elizabeth', 'Peace', 'Tropicana', 'Chrysler Imperial', and several roses that were experimental back when the garden began and we've lost the pedigrees. And we've added many kinds of foxglove, including the rusty type (*Digitalis ferruginea*), the yellow (*D. grandiflora*) and the common purple (*D. purpurea*). There are myriad columbines—the short-spurred pink type that

A clump of *Cleome* 'Helen Campbell' blooms to the right of the bench and various hybrid tea roses bloom amid self-sown sweet alyssum. The pink flowers are *Phlox paniculata* 'Dodo Hanbury Forbes'.

self-sow and are quite long-lived—Siberian and Japanese iris, lots of lupines, globeflowers (*Trollius* spp.), and plenty of annuals mixed in for summer color and for cutting, including cosmos, cleome, snapdragons, and zinnias.

"There is a very large and tall Sargent's weeping hemlock (*Tsuga canadensis* 'Sargentii') in one corner and it appears the cultivar was top-grafted onto a trunk some 6 feet tall. Around the base are *Lobelia cardinalis* 'Whatta Surprise' and throughout the rose garden, alyssums and Johnny jump-ups continue to self-sow, bringing color back every year. There are also armloads of forget-me-nots, their fresh blue color in lovely combination with the roses. The white and pink astilbe were there when I began."

The entire walled area is a rectangle, and standing on a stone terrace in the front of the house you can look down on the garden. After stepping down a 5-foot flight of stone stairs you turn onto a narrow grass terrace that is bounded by another stone wall. Once there you step down in turn to the garden proper. A long stone path runs to the gazebo, itself built into the wall. There are roses on the left and perennials on the right.

To the left of the gazebo is another stone terrace where the garden bench sits. All the stone work is fieldstone set with concrete, and even though the original was close to

Clockwise from lower left, astilbe, *Geranium sanguineum* var. *prostratum*, foxglove (*Digitalis purpurea*), *Campanula latifolia*, a globeflower (*Trollius* spp.), a pink columbine, and a shasta daisy (*Chrysanthemum* × *superbum* 'Little Miss Muffet').

perfection there is still maintenance needed. The walls vary between 5 and 6 to 8 feet high, depending on the slope of the lawn.

There is a little walled-in rock garden overrun in the spring with sweet perfume of lily-of-the-valley (*Convallaria majalis*), the flowers poking their way between and around Japanese pachysandra (*Pachysandra terminalis*). There, under the filtered shade of an old white birch, yellow lady-slippers (*Cypripedium Calceolus* var. *pubescens*) mingle with white trilliums (*Trillium grandiflorum*), while lilac Serbian bellflowers (*Campanula poscharskyana*) and the lovely gold-lace primroses (*Primula* 'Gold Lace')—their petal edges embroidered with gold thread—sparkle in the afternoon sunlight. In one corner are Christmas roses (*Helleborus niger*) that bloom every March.

"One of the main features of the garden," said Ms. Bockbrader, "is a wonderful patch of Japanese primroses (*Primula japonica*) that sit underneath some huge old and warty willows. There are hundreds of them, glowing pink and white. The area is always wet and they have seeded themselves all the way down to the swamp area below."

Robert Frost wrote:

*"Before I built a wall I'd ask to know
What I was walling in or walling out."*

In Mr. Bulkeley's garden, it's obvious to all.

A GARDEN OF ANNUALS

BACK IN THE LATE 1920S, Richardson Wright, for years the editor of *House and Garden* magazine, counted one thousand and eighty-two different types of annual flowers. If, he surmised after much deliberation, he grew twenty-seven of them each year, at the end of forty years he would have seen them all. But that count was made before plant breeders started to really gear up and develop new and bigger cultivars. For a gardener today to see the annuals that are available, even growing thirty-five different ones each year, could possibly take a century.

Charles Goodwin lives in a town called Sherrill. It's a small place in central New York State, incorporated in 1916, and famous as the home of the Oneida Silversmiths. And if any gardener since Richardson Wright has had the chance to know annual flowers, it's Mr. Goodwin. Since 1974 he has grown a total of seven hundred and twenty-three flower cultivars (that's over fifty plants per year) and of these, two hundred and eighteen have made it into his record books with a bloom rating above the average of 21, and with *his* record books that's not an easy thing to do.

"I grade my plants," said Mr. Goodwin, "according to the abundance and duration of their flowers. I use a scale of 0 to 4, in which 0 = no bloom, 1 = scattered bloom, 2 = fair, 3 = they could do better, and 4 = full of bloom. Each Sunday I assess the blossoms of the different cultivars in every one of the twenty beds and record the results in my weekly status report. I start in June and continue to mid-

Left, a colorful patchwork of annuals contains cleomes, celosias, coleus, snapdragons, two kinds of marigolds, and *Silene armeria* 'Royal Electra'. *Above, Pelargonium* 'Sprinter Scarlet', 'Rose Diamond', and 'Gremlin Mix'.

October for eighteen weeks or more, depending on the frosts."

He keeps track of seed sources, the dates of sowing, germination times, when seedlings are transplanted or go out to a cold frame, and the date the plants are set out in the garden.

"I enjoy keeping records," he said. "It helps to pass the long winter nights around here. I keep nine different types of record sheets, ranging from a diagram of bed locations used in planning the gardens, to my weekly status reports.

"And I can look back and find out which were the best flowers in 1978 or in 1983. But according to my records, the wax begonias (*Begonia* × *semperflorens-cultorum*) are the all-time winners. They start blooming in June and hang on until frost. If only they came in some other color besides pink, white, and red!"

Now if Mr. Goodwin merely grew a large number of annuals just for something to enter into his record books, there wouldn't be much of a garden story. But he has an artist's eye. His one-acre lot is a true symphony of color and proves that annuals can do far more than produce lots of flashy blossoms. They can be melded together to become glorious patchworks of color on a quilt of green.

Violet *Delphinium* 'Blue Butterfly' adds contrast to a warm-colored combination of *Impatiens* 'Gem Mix' and 'Princess Light Pink', *Cosmos* 'Sunny Red', and tall-growing *Zinnia* 'Yellow Hornet'.

I asked Mr. Goodwin how he combines colors in his garden.

"I have two approaches," he said. "The flowers either blend well or they make an interesting contrast. I'm not too concerned about the mixing of colors and I think that all garden colors can go together. I prefer not to mix too many reds because they have a tendency to upstage anything you put them next to. My garden as a whole blends all the colors of the rainbow, and I prefer to plant blocks of single colors because they are more dramatic. I let the flowers predict the theme of the garden and I don't use any props or anything fancy; nothing is there to upstage the flowers."

Mr. Goodwin's various gardens have the look of abstract paintings and he mixes the brilliant flowers the way a painter mixes pigments. One particular canvas has a foreground band of red and pink impatiens cultivars, 'Gem Mix' and 'Princess Light Mix'; the middle ground is formed by delphinium 'Blue Butterfly' and cosmos 'Sunny Red'; while a band of tall zinnias, 'Yellow Marvel', brings up the rear. The garden is really an exercise in American abstract impressionism; it is more than a mere collection of flowers.

Another patch contains petunia 'Sugar Plum', with zinnias 'Border Beauty Rose' and 'Pulcino' above and behind. To one side is a mass of reds, pinks, rose, and white provided by dianthus 'Prince' and 'Gaiety'. The bed is topped off by the towering golden-yellow blossoms of *Rudbeckia* 'Double Gold'.

Fourteen years ago Mr. Goodwin retired as foreman for Oneida Silversmiths and began to grow vegetables in his backyard. But soon his wife, Barbara, couldn't cope with all the processing needed to store the harvest. When he had a number of crop failures and also found out who would have to do the work of packaging and freezing all the vegetables, Mr. Goodwin began to grow flowers.

All of the three thousand individual plants that flower in his garden are started anew each year. Even biennials like pansies and chancy perennials like delphiniums are treated like annuals, because nothing except a few trusty perennials are reliably hardy in his Zone 5 garden. And he prefers to start all his plants from seed rather than wintering over begonias, geraniums, and other tender perennials that are often grown as annuals.

The seed-starting process begins in January with slow-growing plants like lisianthus or prairie gentians (*Eustoma grandiflorum*) and geraniums (*Pelargonium* spp.). "By March," he said, "I'm really busy. I use a soilless planting mix and heating cables to provide an even warmth. The hardy annuals are set out in cold frames as soon as the weather permits. I also keep a bank of fluorescent lights going and every year I rig up a temporary greenhouse out of plastic sheeting and heat it by running a hot-air duct out from the basement furnace."

Even though Mr. Goodwin takes extra precautions, including the use of sterilized soil and absolutely clean equipment, there are occasional problems with damping-off, the fungus disease that often attacks emergent seedlings. "Under the lights," he said, "I keep the plants from being overcrowded and make sure there is plenty of air circulation. But I lost some cosmos that gave up the ghost this morning for no known reason. It seems to be a curse from beyond."

The usual date of the last frost in this part of New York is about May 25. Up until that date, the tender plants are in cold frames. But nature can be fickle, and Mr. Goodwin remembers the spring of 1978 when a sudden cold snap had him scurrying around on May 28 tucking the tender plants under sheets of burlap and anything else he could find.

Mr. Goodwin usually doesn't water his garden because he refuses to pamper the plants too much. He weeds, stakes them up if they need it, and gets rid of insect pests. The only fertilizer he uses is leaf mold, and he spreads 2 to 3 inches of composted leaves every other year on the lower beds where the soil is rich in silt, and every year in the upper beds where the clay is thick. The only other thing he uses on the garden is bonemeal. He felt he was getting low on phosphorus in 1987, so that year he spread 2 pounds of bonemeal to each 100 square feet of garden. If the nitrogen level stays relatively low, that's alright because he wants lots of flowers. He keeps the soil pH about 7.0.

For cultivating the soil, he uses a tiller in the fall and on a few occasions in the spring. "But," he laughed, "I've since learned that when you till the ground in the spring, you pull up a whole new crop of weed seeds so I'm using that as an excuse for only doing it in the fall."

Even though Mr. Goodwin has a world of flowers at his beck and call, he is hesitant about cutting them for bouquets. Since he evaluates the plants throughout the season, he wants a good, overall picture of their performances. But he has made a few concessions and allows some asters and snapdragons for cutting.

How does he feel about cultivars designated as All-America Selections? "Well," he mused, "Some are very good and some really don't respond too well. And there are some fine old varieties—a double grandiflora petunia called 'Blushing Maid' comes to mind—that are available for years and then suddenly disappear from the marketplace. That I find is a continual disappointment. But on the whole, most of the All-American Selections are very good. And I make mistakes, too. I wasn't too impressed by the new creeping zinnia, *Sanvitalia procumbens* 'Mandarin Orange' at the beginning of the season, but then I found it to be a continual bloomer right into the fall and it made a great groundcover, too."

As to favorite flowers, he said, "Picking favorite flowers for me is like trying to pick out your favorite child: They all have their good points. But you might say I'm partial to pansies, and to prairie gentians, of course, but I think that the hybridizers have taken some of their vitality away in return for bigger blossoms; and, believe it or not, I still like marigolds."

When you have chance to talk with a dedicated gardener like Mr. Goodwin, you have to ask him at least one question about the weather: What does he do when it rains?

"Well," he pondered for a moment, and then said, "I swear a lot, I guess, and find jobs to do inside that I've put off for several years. Then I remind myself that we need the rain, and then I grouse around for awhile. But eventually the sun comes out again, and like everyone else in the world who really loves flowers, it's back to the garden."

A COLLECTOR'S GARDEN

You exist in a world of speed as you drive across the Tappan Zee Bridge where six lanes of traffic—three one way and three the other—rush across the Hudson River. Upon leaving the bridge you join an onslaught of cars on the New England Throughway that are racing to Connecticut on one side and New York City on the other. Jets zoom overhead and potholes abound below. At last you leave the mayhem of the superhighways for a brief ride on the Hutchinson River Parkway—a road designed for both cars and horsepower of forty years ago—until finally you turn off at the Larchmont exit.

Larchmont is on Long Island Sound and was first developed in 1845, incorporated in 1891, and was home for many years to Joyce Kilmer. After a few comparatively peaceful miles on a local town road, you reach the turnoff that leads to the home of Harold Epstein. And reminiscent of Kilmer's poem, the first thing you notice about the Epstein grounds are the trees: It's an oasis of landscaped green, a rock-bedecked garden that even in the middle of March shows its beauty.

The basic skeleton of the garden is a backbone of rock, marvelous natural granite rock outcroppings—you can see the drill holes in the rock alongside the house where they had to blast to put in a driveway—and then more rocks that were moved into position without benefit of backhoes and tractors, set in place by the hand of man. When the land was originally cleared, fourteen big trees were

Left, rhododendrons, azaleas, and other evergreens: center front, *Buxus microphylla* 'Kingsville Dwarf'; center, *Rhododendron kiusianum* 'Alba'. Above, *Primula sieboldii* and *Arisaema sikokianum.*

Top, Cypripedium calceolus var. parviflorum. Bottom, Epimedium × youngianum 'Niveum' is planted along stone steps.

taken down and some of the rock outcroppings were blasted open to provide pits for planting. And so skillfully has the planting proceeded that you cannot tell which plants seeded themselves and which have wound up in their places as a result of the gardener's hand.

There is, for example, a marvelous stunted white pine that seems to grow directly from a crack in a rock; it looks so natural I complimented Mr. Epstein on planting it there. He smiled and told me he does not know where it came from and nobody in the neighborhood has any of this particular species.

Spring bulbs, including tiny daffodils (*Narcissus asturiensis*) were blooming in various rock crevices when I visited the garden, while below them the snowdrops (*Galanthus* spp.) and winter aconite (*Eranthis hyemalis*) were all in flower, many of them self-seeding right into the gravel edge of the driveway.

The soaring trunks of two oaks (one black and one red) on the front lawn stand to either side of the front door and turn out to be merely poles for the self-clinging, climbing hydrangea (*Hydrangea anomala* subsp. *petiolaris*). The hydrangea on the right oak is the typical form, but Mr. Epstein jumped up in the air to obtain a bit of last year's now-dried flowers and pointed out how much larger is the plant on the left-hand tree.

"This one," he said, "is the 'Skyland' cultivar recognized by Tom Everett some thirty years ago and far the more beautiful of the two."

Asked about his garden, Mr. Epstein said: "I call it my compost heap or graveyard of plants as it contains the greatest variety of plants of all kinds you can imagine. I've been an experimentalist, particularly on the subject of hardiness of plants that will grow in this area. And remember that you only see the live ones; I never boast about the dead ones."

We talked about the hardiness of plants.

The front of the
house, with
blossoming azaleas
and *Tsuga
canadensis
'Pendula'.

"Gardeners in this eastern area," he said, "must contend with the torrid heat of summer and the frigid deep freeze of winter. Yet I've found there are two sets of plants that will flourish: one group represents the eastern natives (including many from the Southeast and the mountains of the southern states) and the other is the Japanese. So this garden is now at least 75 percent to 80 percent Japanese plants (I include eastern Asia and China) with the balance mainly from our area and just a few that have accommodated themselves yet hail from other parts of this country or the world."

Yet even though the roll call of plants would be predominantly Japanese, this is not a Japanese garden by any stretch of the imagination. The look of rocks, the dirty gray cast of a March sky, and the twinkling colors of the spring flowers all look American. When I realized just how many tiny white labels were poking helter-skelter from the still-frosty ground, I realized that if there is a term for it, this must be a collector's garden.

"There are certain plants I cannot grow here," Mr. Epstein continued. "I thought I had an advantage with the woodlands and the elevation of a couple of hundred feet above sea level. Yes, indeed, it's a wonderful climate—we often don't get a frost here until December. But it's a disadvantage because the plants do not harden off and things that people can grow one mile

away from here I just can't grow. They live on land closer to sea level and get earlier frosts."

Once or twice over the years, the Epstein garden has seen temperatures of 8 or 10 degrees below zero, and almost every year without fail they hit 0°F. "But it's not only the bottom line of the thermometer," he said, "it's the prolonged length of freezing cold and the depth of frost in the ground. Many broadleaved evergreens become desiccated because of an inability to pull up moisture from the frozen ground."

Watering problems have been solved in this garden with the installation of buried pipes that run to the base of tall trees, leave the ground to run inconspicuously up the trunk, and end with a rotating spray nozzle at the top so the water falls evenly over all the garden instead of both striking and dripping from leaf to leaf, the expected result if sprinklers were placed among the shrubs below.

As we walked about the garden and looked at the burgeoning buds of spring I marveled at the numerous paths that wound between the rocks and gave the impression of a vast park rather than a mere acre and a half.

"This is a very large garden on a small piece of land," I said.

"Thank God!" he answered. "People say to me, 'Too bad you can't extend your boundaries.' I don't want that because I would just be driven to fill it up with more plants. I have been in this house and garden for fifty-one years and have been planting things every year without exception, irrespective of continually being out of space. We kill off some old plants we're tired of and replace them with the new. I have plants being shipped in over the next few weeks and I don't know where I'm going to put them. I walk around with a plant for a couple of hours before I can find an empty spot because the place is saturated with plants."

He stopped in front of a bush with a very old-looking trunk and tiny buds, dark purple against the brown of the bark.

"Know what this is?" he asked.

"I do. It's an *Abeliophyllum distichum*, but surely the oldest I've ever seen."

"It's about thirty-five years old. Some twenty-five years ago I tried to get a local nurseryman interested in that shrub. Told him he could take cuttings. He didn't think it would be worth the effort. Now he carries this shrub every season. Suddenly it's popular."

We walked into the greenhouses.

"I once had a lot of orchids but had to give up something as there is only so much time. Over here are some beautiful plants."

A shelf held many pots, most of them arisaemas from Japan, all in bloom. They looked vaguely like the faces found on the carved wooden pipes of the dwarfs' pump organ in *Snow White and the Seven Dwarfs*. Some of the blossoms were on tall stems, some were short, some were pale green, one almost white, and one a deep maroon, and all had the canopy that we expect to see sheltering Jack. They resemble our Jack-in-the-pulpit (*Arisaema triphyllum*) but somehow keep that touch of the exotic that one expects in plants from Japan.

On another shelf were pots of a graceful green grass.

"That's the parent species of *Hakonechola macra* 'Aureola', almost as attractive as the grass we find so beautiful in our gardens."

We walked about the garden for a few minutes more. A wan late-winter sun began to shine through the overcast. The spring flowers sparkled with a new intensity and I took to my car and left a pocket of solitude and rather sadly retraced my way to the afternoon world of highways and speed.

A GARDEN IN MANHATTAN

YEARS AGO I THOUGHT that the best life that an artist could live would be found atop a sky-scraper in Manhattan, where I would sing the tunes of Gordon Jenkin's musical vignette *Manhattan Tower* and dream of a garden with graceful flowers and trees whose branches would bend out over a parapet in the winds that blew from spire to spire. I knew there were gardens in Manhattan that ranged from the formal tracings of ivy, holly, and rhodo-dendrons next to the vestry of Grace Epis-copal Church on Broadway and Tenth Street to the myriad tubs of annuals arranged across the open courts in the front of so many brownstones.

So it was no surprise for me to discover, some years ago, that Ken Druse, garden writer and photographer, had installed him-self atop a seven story building in Manhat-tan's art center of SoHo (an acronym for "South of Hou-ston" Street) and pro-ceeded to establish a garden. The surprise was the lushness of the plants all growing in a climate which is said to be the south-ern boundary of Zone 6 but which, because of the cold winds that blow between the buildings in winter and the torrid temperatures from the sun and from radiant heat reflected from neighbor-ing rooftops in summer, is more like a desert in Arizona.

Left, the garden in summer includes white *Rosa* 'Iceberg', behind it a red hibiscus standard summering outdoors, *Monarda didyma* 'Cambridge Scarlet' in the foreground, behind it purple loosestrife and liatris, and yellow *Hemerocallis* 'Hyperion'. *Above,* morning glory 'Heavenly Blue'.

"Gardening in the sky," said Mr. Druse, "differs greatly from gardening on the earth. Soil, for example, doesn't have to be improved—it must be imported, and the hope of every rooftop gardener is a good elevator system. The plants must grow in restrictive containers and are constantly exposed to soot and pollution, as well as being at nature's mercy. And they must suffer through winters that often lack the protection of snow cover. Buffeted by wind, my poor trees would leaf out two to three weeks later than the same varieties on the ground and show autumn colors weeks earlier than their cousins at sea level."

The roof of the 100-year-old building is vaulted brick and can support vast amounts of weight. But in spite of this, Mr. Druse took the precaution to consider the weight factors of both soil and containers, siting the heavier planters over supporting beams.

"I can't overly stress the importance of this," he said. "One tree in a 14-inch container full of soil is heavy; I had one that weighed in at 250 pounds. Six of them in one spot could weigh up to several hundred pounds and if someone installed a raised bed directly on the roof it could wind up weighing a ton or more. Many rooftops were not made to hold this kind of load so you must check your building's structure before starting such a garden."

The planting medium was also developed for considerations of weight. It is an adjustable ratio that averages three parts peat moss to one part perlite—more perlite for plants that like a fast-draining medium, and less for moisture lovers. Each container got an additional 2-inch layer of perlite at the bottom for drainage. Although the potting mix is very light and holds much more moisture than garden loam, it provides no nutrition. That is supplied by fertilizers.

The containers are arranged in rows surrounding a small deck area so that the garden covers 1500 square feet of the 80- by 100-foot roof. Most of the containers are made from oak whiskey barrels sawed in half, with eight or more half-inch drainage holes drilled into the bottoms. They are coated inside and out with a wood preservative that is nontoxic to plants.

"In spring," said Mr. Druse, "I fertilize with a granular, commercial preparation that is low in nitrogen, to discourage hard-to-maintain vegetative growth, and high in phosphorous, to encourage both flowers and fruit. After the initial feeding, food is siphoned directly into the watering system every other week until August. Feeding ends early to temper growth and promote hardening for the coming winter and improve the plants' tolerance to the biting winds."

In a garden such as this, watering becomes the most demanding of tasks. Because he might be called away at a moment's notice for an assignment, Mr. Druse was forced to design an automated system of timers and valves that controls three sections of the roof. Large tubes the size of a garden hose branch off with smaller hose "capillaries" that end with spot-spitters or dribble-rings (names that sound more like laugh-getting articles in a catalog of joke items than watering devices) in each container.

"The large tubes," he said, "are laid in place and holes are punched along their length. Then the smaller capillary hoses are inserted. The plastic used is 'self-healing,' closing around each tube to make a leak-proof connection. Two different emission sizes control the flow and every day during July and August, each section of the garden is watered for ten minutes, starting just before dawn. I adapted the system from various patio and lawn irrigation supplies. The system is quite simple, inexpensive, and it only took me a few hours to connect.

"But that isn't all there is to it. To protect the typical tar-paper roof usually found on these buildings, I laid a grid of pressure-treated two-by-fours following the direction to the roof's drains. All of the containers are elevated on this grid, allowing water to drain and air to circulate

beneath. There are also two raised platforms that create a tiered effect, and since most trees and shrubs stop growing when their roots fill a container these staged areas exaggerate height."

Among the trees and shrubs that took rooftop conditions in their stride were the following American natives: green ash (*Fraxinus pennsylvanica*), staghorn sumac (*Rhus typhina*), pussy willow (*Salix discolor*), oak-leaved hydrangea (*Hydrangea quercifolia*), honey locust (*Glesitsia triacanthos*), and two imports, the tamarisk (*Tamarix ramosissima*) and European white birch (*Betula pendula*).

To soften the look of the various containers, Mr. Druse planted vines, with flowering varieties used to cover screens and twig trellises. Here, too his choices are imaginative, using the American honeysuckle (*Lonicera sempervirens*) and the Virginia creeper (*Parthenocissus quinquefolia*)—its autumn color is spectacular—plus Boston ivy (*Parthenocissus tricuspidata*) and two groundcovers, Kenilworth ivy (*Cymbalaria muralis*) and ground ivy (*Glechoma hederacea*). For a tropical look he chose mandevilla (*Mandevilla* × *amabilis* 'Alice du Pont'). "I built," he said, "a rooftop greenhouse over a skylight opening where I can winter the subtropical pot plants."

"For a long season of color," he said, "I stick to easy-care perennials that do well in containers. And I found that, quite surprisingly, peonies will do well in containers, proving them to be tougher than I ever thought them to be. For interest in the autumn, I started with the ornamental grasses. One of my favorites is ravenna grass (*Erianthus ravennae*); its silvery plumes rise 8 to 10 feet into the air and can easily be dried for winter bouquets."

Other ornamental grasses in the skytop garden are fountain grass (*Pennisetum setaceum*), a particularly graceful form of the eulalia grass (*Miscanthus sinensis* 'Gracillimus') that boasts thin and curving leaves with a white midrib, and the striped zebra grass, the striking tropical-looking cultivar of the Miscanthus tribe (*M. sinensis* 'Zebrinus').

Perennials in the rooftop garden include the following native American wildflowers: beebalm (*Monarda didyma*), Carolina phlox (*Phlox carolina* 'Miss Lingard'), false indigo (*Baptisia australis*), gay-feather (*Liatris spicata*), Joe-Pye weed (*Eupatorium maculatum*), and bleeding-heart (*Dicentra spectabilis*), a plant which most Americans call their own but which originally came from Japan. "And of course I included the American coneflower (*Echinacea purpurea*) and dozens of gloriosa daisies (*Rudbeckia hirta* 'Gloriosa Daisy').

"Most people," said Mr. Druse, "who indulge in rooftop gardening content themselves with a few evergreens, including a yew or two, a prostrate juniper and perhaps if the muse gets them, a Japanese black pine. But I wanted more than that, I wanted *color*. And I knew that many of the wildflowers survive in nature with little in the way of soil and a lot in the way of weather."

Other perennials in Mr. Druse's garden include the tawny daylily (*Hemerocallis fulva*)—naturalized now all over America but originally an escapee from the gardens of European and English settlers—and a species of yarrow (*Achillea filipendulina*).

For annuals Mr. Druse chooses only those that will continue to bloom without deadheading or those that will reseed year after year. High on his list are the cornflower or

The garden in its first year, shown here, was already full of color.

bachelor's button (*Centaurea Cyanus*) and globe amaranth (*Gomphrena globosa*).

"In the early years of the garden, my years of living in New England had led me to dream of growing vegetables, an urban skytop farm. But believe it or not, the air around Manhattan throngs with insects and many of them are the enemy. Every August, for example, the tomato hornworms find their way to the crowded skies and immediately spy my crop. So in order to harvest any of my tiny tomatoes ('Sweet One Hundred') I have to keep an eagle eye. I also grow 'Sugar Snap' peas and one short variety of corn, 'Butterfruit', that makes a magnificent sight as you gaze at the Empire State Building through its nodding tassels. But you need a lot of corn plants because the high winds blow much of the needed pollen out to the sky."

He has been successful with fruits as well, and grows a good crop of raspberries, especially the variety 'Fall Gold'.

"Ultimately," said Mr. Druse, "the deciding factor to the worthiness of any plant forced to live in a container is whether it survives or not; the plants that couldn't make it in my garden are gone. But every spring when the garden awakens from its winter slumbers, I realize there is nothing like a garden and thank heaven for the fortitude of those plants that delight in living in the sky."

A GARDEN IN
THE GARDEN STATE

Just about twenty two miles due west of Manhattan's Forty-second Street lies the New Jersey town of Madison. First settled in 1715, the town was called Bottle Hill until 1834, incorporated in 1889, and is the home of Drew University. The city is close to the Great Swamp, a 7,000-acre hardwood swamp of marsh and open water that is host to two hundred species of birds. and twice that in seed plants and ferns. Since 1965 the swamp has been a National Wildlife Refuge and Wilderness Area, in part due to the efforts of Florence and Robert Zuck, who served with the original band of people who were dedicated to saving the vast wetlands from being filled in to serve as a potential airport.

In addition to their efforts in saving the Great Swamp, the Zucks were involved in establishing both the Frelinghuysen Arboretum (headquarters of the Morris County park system) and as Drew faculty members (with the cooperation of the Garden Club of Madison), the Drew Forest Preserve. The preserve is a small remnant of the vast forest which covered eastern North America before the European settlers invaded the continent. The Zucks were honored upon their retirement from teaching in 1980 when the Trustees of Drew designated approximately ten acres of the forest preserve as the Florence and Robert Zuck Arboretum.

"We have been involved in conservation," said Mrs. Zuck, "since coming to New Jersey. The problem is that not enough people do become involved. Many more are needed."

Left, the perennial bed aglow with chartreuse lady's mantle, pink astilbes, and blue delphiniums.
Above, irises and Rocky Mountain columbines bloom beneath a sweet bay magnolia.

Another view of
the perennial bed.
The gray plants are
lamb's-ears
(*Stachys byzantina*).

But it's not only for their public works that the Zucks are known. They also have a private garden located fast by the Drew Forest Preserve, where twenty-four kinds of ferns grow (they run the gamut from the common but sweet-smelling hay-scented fern *(Dennstaedtia punctilobulia)* to the beautiful golden-green woodfern or Goldie's fern *(Dryopteris Goldiana)*. All those ferns grow in proximity to a collection of over sixty wildflowers. There, in a garden alive with the sound of bird songs in the spring and often visited by the little wood satyr butterfly, glorious wandflowers *(Galax aphylla)* bloom in company with the shy yellow flowers of the sessile bellwort *(Uvularia sessilifolia)* and the may-apple *(Podophyllum peltatum)*.

"Although most of the plants are wild," said Mrs. Zuck, "we mixed in many different species of herbaceous and woody plants including asters *(Aster* spp.), goldenrods *(Solidago* spp.), azaleas, anemones, bloodroot *(Sanguinaria canadensis)*, and the beautiful *Shortia galacifolia*, along with the ferns."

Even though the Zucks are both retired from active teaching, the garden is still being used by students who come over from Drew to be introduced to horticulture. Those students interested in forest ecology are especially fortunate to have the Zucks' garden at their disposal—the garden is right at the edge of the Drew Forest Preserve.

Both the Zucks are graduates of Oberlin College, where each majored in botany. They came to Drew in 1946 with two small children and lived in apartments until 1955 when they moved— with two more children—into their newly purchased carriage house that was part of a once-larger estate.

"We did not start with any particular garden in mind," said Mr. Zuck. "We had good soil because the area had been the kitchen garden for the estate. Although there have been many changes over the years, the basic shape of the garden was dictated by the fact that we put almost everything in the front of our two acres because there are only 17 feet of usable space in the rear. The gardens cover about three quarters of an acre and contain some two to three thousand plants."

In the spring the lilacs and the azaleas bloom with lily-of-the-valley in the foreground.

Rows of lamb's-ears, *Iris cristata,* and *Epimedium grandiflorum niveum* lead the eye to the sundial in the garden's center.

Rings of creeping blue phlox (*Phlox divaricata*) and primroses (*Primula vulgaris*) surround the ivy-covered gray birch.

They cut down many dead elms, both seedling and sapling silver, red, and sugar maples, but they saved a patch of second growth hickory, oak, cherry, birch, and sassafras, the location where most of the wild plants now grow.

The more formal perennial garden is built around a copy of an antique sundial. "We needed a focal point for that area and the sundial fitted perfectly," said Mrs. Zuck. Here the chartreuse froth of Lady's mantle (*Alchemilla vulgaris*) blends with the royal blue of delphiniums (*Delphinium grandiflorum*) and the hot pinks of astilbes (*Astilbe* spp.), including the cultivars 'Betsy Cuperus' in pink and 'Europa' for red. The visitor can walk a green path lined with the lovely gray leaves of lamb's ears (*Stachys byzantina,* once known as *S. lanata*).

The formal garden is enclosed with seventy-five boxwoods (*Buxus* spp.) all the progeny of one original cutting donated by Florence's sister, who then lived in Virginia. Some of the shrubs are now forty years old.

The Zucks have left standing several old gray birch volunteers (*Betula populifolia*) that form an alley of great charm. I say "left" because this stalwart and gracefully bending tree—it will grow where so many others perish—is often doomed by landscapers, who usually refer to it as an inferior tree and recommend instead the white birch (*B. papyrifera*). There is also a smaller and younger group of birches at the beginning of the wild garden, their off-white bark clothed with a luxuriant growth of small-leaved English ivy (*Hedera Helix*), surrounded in the spring by blooming Jacob's ladder (*Polemonium reptans*) and a number of primrose hybrids.

The Zucks are among the precious few people of this world who recognize the quote by Goethe, "To know of someone here and there whom we accord with, who is living on with us, even in silence—this makes our earthly ball a peopled garden."

AN ELEGANT GARDEN FOR ALL SEASONS

To paraphrase Samuel Johnson: Whoever wishes to attain an English style must be familiar but not coarse, and elegant but not ostentatious. Nowhere is that line more amply illustrated than in the gardens of Dr. James and Janet Hester. For it is difficult to believe that when walking the brick paths that wind between banks of shrubbery, shaded by two European beech trees that date from the nineteenth century and having the mind's eye refreshed by the ivies, hostas, and English box  hedges that line the walks, visitors are only 50 miles away from the fervored glitz of midtown Manhattan. This garden stands on ground that was involved in the Revolutionary War in January 1777, when George Washington and his troops defeated a large British force here after the battle of Trenton.

Asked how he happened to begin gardening, Dr. Hester said: "In 1980, we returned from a five-year sojourn in Japan when I became President of the New York Botanical Garden. I was, to put it mildly, greatly stimulated by that position. We moved back into our old house that stood on one acre of land and included an eight-year-old, well-established backyard garden. But I wanted to create a variety of "rooms," a theme often found in many English gardens, especially at Hidcote and Sissinghurst. So with the help of Robert Zion and Yuji Yoshimura we redesigned many areas, ending up with a Japanese garden, a

Left, looking across the island bed with yucca toward the formal perennial garden in midwinter.
Above, the island bed in summer.

The Japanese
garden in
midwinter.

fern and wildflower walk, a hosta bed, and perennial beds."

Although the garden reflects both England and Japan, it does so in a very American way, chiefly because of the climate along the eastern seaboard. Even though the Atlantic Ocean is about twenty-five miles away, winters are often severe and temperatures in the garden have been known to reach 0°F. Yet winter is one time of the year that the Hester garden is often quite beautiful.

Under a lacy covering of freshly fallen snow, the paths of the formal perennial garden turn to white. Baltic ivy (*Hedera helix* 'Baltica') is the hardy and evergreen groundcover that forms a carpet both for the statue at the rear and the island bed with its yucca (*Yucca glauca*) centerpiece. Behind the statue—itself a relic from the early twentieth century when the site was the residence of Woodrow Wilson—is a bank of Japanese holly (*Ilex crenata* 'Convexa').

"The garden is beautiful in winter," said Dr. Hester, "but as with most American gardens, it is truly at its best about the middle of May."

It is then that the greens are offset by the magnificent blooms of a peony bed and a mass of Montauk daisies (*Chrysanthemum nipponicum*). From April to June color accents are provided by a playful mix of white and blue pansies, then for summer a mix of heliotrope (*Heliotropum* 'Blue Marine') and hot pink petunias.

The Japanese garden is highlighted with a stone lantern that is surrounded by an azalea cultivar, 'Satsuki,' the dwarf Japanese juniper (*Juniperus procumbens* 'Nana')—a marvelous miniature introduced to America in 1904 by the Hill Nursery of Dundee, Illinois—dwarf Alberta spruce (*Picea glauca* var. *albertiana*), along with *Malus* 'Red Jade', the marvelous weeping crab apple discovered by the Brooklyn Botanic Garden some fifty years ago.

Another trick to the elegance of this garden is the swimming pool. Instead of an open tile trench lined with sapphire blue and completely at odds with everything except the greenest of grasses, the Hesters have a 35-foot black concrete swimming circle that looks for all the world like a reflecting pool and acts as a design element all through the year.

All in all, I'm very sure that Dr. Johnson—had he been allowed to visit—would have been completely at home.

PENNSYLVANIA ROCK GARDEN

HAWLEY, PENNSYLVANIA IS A typical small town. Its main street is wide, with room for parked cars on either side, and it supports a working Victorian hotel, an authentic '30s diner, a railroad track (only at one end) and, nestled between tree-covered hills, a small grid of tree-lined side streets with well-cared-for homes. The fishing is fine in the spring, baseball reigns all summer long, and every fall hunters journey from Philadelphia to try for their first buck in the thick forest that begins just the other side of the town line.

Just east of the town proper, high on one particular hill, a few small homes are perched on the hillside. One particular house on a two-acre lot boasts a small clearing, some 2,500 square feet carved out of living rock, that easily holds thousands of individual plants and over six hundred rare and unusual species from literally every corner of the world. It is the rock garden of L. Budd Myers.

My first visit to the garden left me speechless for an hour. There was no way on that sunny day in June to prepare for the carefully worked patchwork quilt of color that existed half a mile from the A & P and a mile from the hotel.

"There's much more color in early May," said Mr. Myers. "Last winter we had enough snow cover to protect many of the more tender alpines and the fence held back the usual onslaught of deer. I woefully discovered months after the rock garden was underway that it was created in the path of a

---

Left, along the edge of the garden a yellow pea tree, *Caragana arborescens* forma *lorbergii* blooms above a remarkable assortment of dwarf conifers and other flowering plants. *Above, Campanula cochlearifolia.*

Top, Daphne arbuscula *and yellow* Sedum stelliforme. *Bottom, blazing star or fairy wand,* Chamaelirium luteum.

deer run. The fence is a hateful but necessary limitation; it did stop the plants from being mangled by deer hooves."

We walked to the large natural rock outcrop, just back of the center of the garden, where I saw a blooming eastern bear grass (*Xerophyllum asphodeloides*) below the edge of the rock. "That only blooms every other year at best, but this is the finest it's been in recent memory," Mr. Myers said. He arched his hand over his left shoulder as he looked down the hill. "Up there is the pea tree (*Caragana arborescens* forma *Lorbergii*) and some of the wildflower collections. Down to our left, at the bottom, is the bog garden. Along the old rock wall I've put invasive plants like *Coreopsis verticillata*, a tickseed.

"Starting up from the bottom right are many plants collected in the western states—there are some dozen species of columbine here (*Aquilegia* spp.). Directly to our right is a collection of a dozen cold-hardy rabbit-eared cacti (*Opuntia* spp.) from the Great Plains, and a few other types of plants from that area.

"I started fifteen years ago," he continued, "with a bulldozer hired for the day. We cleared all the soil from the tops of the rock outcrops—the driver was a bit confused by the whole thing—and put all the collected soil to one side. The garden became rather like a small square amphitheater, with the rocks becoming the tiers of seats and the point at the center of the old stone wall being the open arena. After the big digging was over, then I started on my own. I covered all the areas that would not get immediate treatment with black plastic to kill existing weeds and to keep more from sprouting. I trucked in gravel from a nearby bank. Then, working with a general mix of sand, gravel, peat moss, some composted soil and a dash of powdered manure, I began to move in fill. The first plants to enter the garden were dwarf evergreens to create fo-

cal points: hemlocks, spruces, and rhododendrons."

It was beginning to get warm by now, the sun heating the tops of the gravel chips and the areas of bare rock, so I asked about watering.

"I rarely water," he said. "This is a weekend garden; it must be on its own—often for two weeks or more—without much help from me. The topdressing of small gravel chips that covers the entire garden acts as mulch to preserve moisture. During the winter months, the garden is also on its own. Years without snow always take their toll of plants, but the majority usually recover."

"And," he added, "under the walkway at the very lowest center of the garden, I installed a system of perforated drainpipes that are embedded in the gravel fill so water can never stand or stagnate."

Looking down toward the stone wall, I said that although the garden was only 50 by 50 feet, it never seemed small or overly crowded; there always seemed to be room for more.

"The levels of rock help to give the garden breathing room," he said. "I've had to prune a few dwarf conifers over the years when they grew enough to block out a view—it's easy to forget that even if a plant only grows an inch a year, when you're dealing with a limited space the ten-year total can make a statement."

"I've tried to shy away from hard and fast rules," he explained. "You remember: don't put a shocking pink next to a bright red, etc. But when you're dealing with a world of alpines and the like, it's impossible to tone most of them down." He pointed to a new lily blooming at the foot of the wall. "Speaking of intensity, that will have to go. It's called 'Headlight' and it sure is;

much too bright next to grey rock. Oh, it will never be finished; a garden is a living thing. And plants die. You would not believe the number of plants that have not survived or seeds that never germinated."

Seeds are one of the clues to the complexities of Mr. Myers' garden. For many years he has belonged to various alpine and rock garden societies both here and in England and Scotland. It is by the judicial use of the various seed exchanges that he has been able to build such a vast collection of plants.

"It's easier to start from seed," he said. "Aside from the sheer excitement of shepherding a plant from seed to flowering, it gives a plant the opportunity to adapt to differences between here and its original home, whether that's in the Himalaya Mountains or Kew Gardens. And there are differences. I've often felt that if a plant can survive the rigors of the Northeast, it can do well most anywhere. We can never predict snow cover, amount of rainfall, or temperatures from week to week. Last year was going to be the worst winter in a decade and instead it was very, very mild. Then there were the rains this year.

"Starting plants from seed and bringing them on has been one of the goals: it's sometimes satisfying, always interesting. But creating the appropriate settings within this small rock garden has tended to be the astonishing outcome of needs imposed by the plants themselves."

"And you never know what is blooming right over the next hill, he continued as we walked over to a small cleft in the rocks and bent down to see a diminutive jack-in-the-pulpit, a 3-inch blossom on a 6-inch plant.

Just to our left a cloud of candy-striped lewisia (*Lewisia cotyledon* 'Sunset Strain') blossoms began to move in a slight breeze, unaware that they were no longer in the mountains in Oregon; to our right a group of American columbine (*Aquilegia canadensis*) perched over a bed

of *Aurinia saxatilis* (formerly *Alyssum saxatile*) 'Citrinum', while a few steps more took us to a large bed of *Haberlea rhodopensis* in full bloom, gently nestled against a clump of Japanese painted fern (*Athyrium goeringianum* 'Pictum').

We followed the path past the mounds of tufa rock, brilliant with the bright yellows of *Draba rigida* and *Douglasia vitaliana* down to the small bog garden.

"I planted an old concrete-stoppered bathtub here," said Myers. "I added a rotted log and filled it with thoroughly soaked peat moss, then, as in the rest of the garden, started most of the bog plants from seed. The first plant used was truthfully a minor reason for the establishment of the bog. It was a *Geum pentapetalum*, in turn raised from one seed that alone germinated from a seed exchange packet of many years ago. Before the bog, it languished for several years in the scree, but now, after moving it to the lip of the tub, the shrublet has thrived and gnarled itself into a splendid natural bonsai."

There are sharp inclines on either side of the buried tub, held back by a naturalistic wall of squarish rocks that edge the bog to make it a level below the rest of the garden—a manmade, cirquelike basin.

I looked over the garden, still amazed by the many different plants around me. Then I noticed an empty spot of dirt way over to the right, close to the fence. It was about 3 feet square and very conspicuous now that I became aware of it. I asked what grew there.

"Nothing yet," answered Mr. Myers. "It was recently reclaimed from a stand of sedums that went wild and is now ready for a few choice plants from next year's crop of seedlings."

Like all great gardens, Budd Myers' rock garden will never be finished. It continues to evolve and change with each passing season.

A BUCKS COUNTY GARDEN

THE HAMLET OF LAHASKA, Pennsylvania, is situated at the headwaters of Lahaska Creek, about one mile from Lahaska Station, and some nine miles from the spot where Washington crossed the Delaware River on Christmas night of 1776 to defeat the British at Trenton, New Jersey. Lahaska is an Indian name that means "meeting of the springs," and many of the houses in the area are over 200 years old.

Earl Hart Jamison has lived and gardened in this particular spot in Lahaska for only five years. He mows about ten acres of land and has flowers in beds and borders scattered throughout. The property was originally a farm and although Mr. Jamison admits to liking flowers, he is very fond of vegetables, especially when he can eat

them right out of his garden.

He grows lots of annuals and perennials and only plants what will give the most effect with the least amount of maintenance.

"Certain plants seem to stand up under any climatic conditions. I don't bother with petunias—they continually wilt in the summer heat unless you are ready with the hose or watering can. I do like bedding begonias (*Begonia × semperflorens-cultorum*)—I call them the workhorse of my garden—and I like ageratums (*Ageratum Houstonianum*). Cleomes or spider flowers (*Cleome Hasslerana*) are, to me, the greatest flower in the world for guaranteeing great effects for the garden. They can transform a standard border design into one that is extra-special."

Left, a mixed bed of perennials and annuals includes a tall, pink-flowered beebalm, white cleomes, and an edging of pink wax begonias, rosy ageratums, yellow marigolds, pink zinnias, and white-leaved dusty miller. Clematis twines arounds the weather vane's pole. *Above*, rhubarb and annuals.

Mr. Jamison has been involved with flowers all his life. Twenty-five years ago he created Peddler's Village, a country-type shopping center that has always been known for its floral displays. Before that he was in the nursery business. As a child his family was in the business of supplying asters for the commercial flower market, and he remembers the time spent packing blossoms in crates for shipment.

As to time spent in his garden today, he freely admits from ten to twelve hours a week during the height of the season. If he gets behind in maintenance he brings in a few people to help with weeding, deadheading, and general cleanup.

There is one view of his garden that features part of a border with a very large and blooming bridal-wreath bush (*Spiraea* spp.), surrounded with peonies and bedding begonias along the edge. For a moment it could pass as an elegant English border until you look closely and notice

An unmistakably American combination of white peonies (in the foreground), a white spiraea, and pink gas plant, with pink peonies and purple irises visible beyond.

that the grass has not been mown and tended for three hundred years and that the stone springhouse in the background and the woods behind are distinctly American both in look and style.

"That stone house," said Mr. Jamison, "is some one hundred and fifty years old and covers the spring and pipes that carry the water down to the original farmhouse. The spiraea is between five and seven years old. I bought it the year we moved in here. I always think that any developing garden should have a few specimen plants to give it a settled look while you wait for everything else to grow. In all my borders I have planted some rather large evergreens that are mixed with deciduous plants for added winter interest. And although we rarely have temperatures below 0°F we still get a lot of winter."

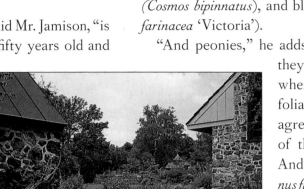

In another part of the grounds there is a paved brick walk that is bordered by a long line of daylilies (*Hemerocallis* spp.). "I blush to say I cannot remember the cultivar name of those plants. I don't document things the way I should. You keep collecting plants but forget to write down their peculiarities. I try to do better but I never do. But when I plan and plant, I try to use everything in a natural manner; all the stone and bricks are used in a rustic fashion and that in itself helps to give a feeling of age to this garden."

As to his other favorite plants, Mr. Jamison admits to loving hostas in all shapes and sizes; he enjoys the brightness of zinnias and the sparkle of the tall varieties of cosmos (*Cosmos bipinnatus*), and blue salvia (*Salvia farinacea* 'Victoria').

"And peonies," he adds. "Not only are they magnificent when in bloom, the foliage is altogether agreeable for the rest of the garden year. And dogwoods (*Cornus florida*), of course. Two years ago I moved in fifty of them with trunk diameters of between 1 1/2 and 3 inches. I was dead certain that I would lose them to that dogwood fungus disease but I sprayed them with a fungicide and watered them well and they look like they will do well this year."

When I asked Mr. Jamison if there were any plants he *doesn't* like, he said, "I don't like German iris in particular; the foliage is not very neat in return for the very short season of flowers.

"Why do I garden? I garden for lots of reasons: Certainly when you grow up with your hands in the soil you can't get away from it. And I'm a business person with all the pressures associated with running a business today. Gardening is such a nice solitary release. You go out by yourself and have the rewards of the flowers and vegetables.

"Vegetables," he sighs. "Did I tell you I love to eat them right out of the garden?"

A GARDEN OF GRASSES

Baltimore, Maryland was settled early in the seventeenth century, but the date of its founding is set at 1729 when the royal governor authorized the building of the town. When the British occupied Philadelphia in 1776, the U.S. Congress was forced to meet in Baltimore. The city was decidedly pro-Southern during the Civil War, and after a disastrous fire in 1904, a new and planned city rose from the ashes.

Jacqueline and Eric Gratz live in a two-story bungalow-style house built in 1905 and covered with gray shingles, that sits in the middle of a half-acre lot in a suburb of Baltimore.

"We moved into the area in 1973," said Mrs. Gratz, "and found a garden that consisted largely of big trees that created a great deal of shade. For the next six years we selectively cleared the land for part of the summer and vacationed in Mt. Desert Island in Maine for the rest. During those vacation days we discovered the waving grasses of sunny meadows and wished to create the same feeling back home."

So the Gratzes approached the landscape architect firm of Oehme, van Sweden & Associates, because of their reputation for naturalistic designs and their continual use of ornamental grasses.

"Both the house and garden," said James van Sweden, "sit close to neighboring houses, so a garden design was needed that would produce screens for privacy without turning the yard into a barricaded fortress. And some of the most successful plants for this purpose are the beautiful ornamental grasses."

Left, to the left of the walk are Sedum Telephium *'Autumn Joy' and behind, the ornamental grass,* Molina caerulea. *The grass at lower right is* Pennisetum orientale. *Above, a bed of* Rudbeckia fulgida *'Goldsturm'.*

Unlike the acid-green clumps of clipped-off leaves, that we generally imagine when we think of grass, these stately perennial garden grasses range from the majestic miscanthus or eulalia grasses (*Miscanthus* spp.) to the ruby-red shades of Japanese blood grass (*Imperata cylindrica rubra*), to the graceful waterless sprays of the fountain grasses (*Pennisetum* spp.). The blades are long or short, wide or thin, and come in all shades of green including the blue green of a number of fescues (*Festuca* spp.).

A bluestone path surrounds the house and enables the garden visitor to walk along and listen to the rustle of the grass leaves in the wind and marvel at the intricacies of the blossoms.

For more color, there are sedums (*Sedum Telephium* 'Autumn Joy'), Siberian bugloss (*Brunnera macrophylla*)—which is beautiful when naturalized among shrubs—and the ligularias (*Ligularia dentata* 'Desdemona'), which bear handsome leaves and golden flowers in the early fall. (Ligularia leaves will wilt in the hot sun even when the roots are in a moist situation, but they recover when the evening cools.) In addition, there are marvelous drifts of *Rudbeckia* 'Goldsturm' surrounded by grasses on either side.

"Plus the astilbes," said Mrs. Gratz. "I love astilbe and have masses of them that, when blooming in early June, make a sea of garnet red under a river birch. And there are many epimediums, as they make such a marvelous groundcover, including *Epimedium* × *rubrum* and 'Sulphureum'."

Although the grasses are desirable for all seasons, they are at their most spectacular in the autumn. Many members of the grass family bear leaves that turn marvelous shades of brown and tan, in colors that glow against the gray skies of fall. Add to the scene in the Gratz garden the

English ivy (*Hedera Helix*) and *Spodiopogon sibiricus* surround a Colorado blue spruce (*Picea pungens* 'Glauca') with *Sedum Telephium* 'Autumn Joy' in the background.

Top, a mix of
ornamental grasses,
rudbeckia, and
lilyturf (*Liriope
Muscari* 'Big Blue')
in early August.
Bottom, another
lilyturf cultivar,
'Variegata', and
Astilbe chinensis
'Pumila' on the left
of the walk with
*Pennisetum
orientale* to the
right.

brilliant orange leaves of a hornbeam (*Car-pinus caroliniana*), the steel-blue needles of the Colorado blue spruces (*Picea pungens*), and the red berries of the hawthornes (*Crataegus* spp.), and you have a scene that Monet could have painted if he had forsworn waterlilies for grasses.

Then there are the seedheads, golden white or iridescent purple plume-like affairs reminiscent of feathers without birds—many resembling the giant fans that slaves used to cool an overheated Cleopatra as she sailed down the Nile in her barge.

Even in winter (the garden is in Zone 7 but on occasion temperatures have dropped to 5° below zero) the leaves and many of the seedheads persist and relieve the monotony of snow. Buffeted and blown by the wind, the leaves are strong enough to persist into spring.

Then they are cut back to make way for the coming season's new growth.

"Maintenance for this garden," said Mrs. Gratz, "consists of going out into the yard late in the winter—along about the end of February or the beginning of March—with a sharpened shears and chopping away the brown stalks of the grasses. Then we sit back and enjoy the spring bulbs, and by the time their leaves are turning brown the grasses are up and growing, hiding the ripening foliage of the bulbs."

Among the grasses in the Gratz garden are feather reed grass (*Calamagrostis acutiflora stricta*), maiden grass (*Miscanthus sinensis* 'Gracillimus'), *Miscanthus sinensis purpurascens*—an early bloomer with reddish foliage—and two fountain grasses, *Pennisetum alopecuroides* and *P. oriental*.

Because of the plantings, the Gratzes enjoy a phenomenal amount of wildlife in the garden. "We have in this strict suburban area," Mrs. Gratz said, "a red fox. He leaves his distinct odor among the grasses over the winter. And we've seen him at the blueberry bushes where he has had an altercation with a raucous mockingbird. We have many different birds, especially during the fall migrations. There are always white-throated and song sparrows and juncos feeding on the seeds of the *Pennisetum alopecuroides*. You can see the grasses bob up and down as the birds go at the seeds.

"Most of the trees and shrubs were chosen to attract birds. The Devil's walking-stick (*Aralia spinosa*) is especially attractive to the flickers, the rosebreasted grosbeaks, and the wood and hermit thrushes."

There is a traditional Wexford curse that states: "May the grass grow at your door and the fox build his nest on your hearthstone." If the Gratzes' fox stays in the grass, I'm sure they can take the curse as a compliment.

A PAINTER'S GARDEN

NEWPORT NEWS IS ON the coast of southeastern Virginia. It is one of the ports of the Hampton Roads, an area of water through which the James, Nansemond, and Elizabeth Rivers empty into Chesapeake Bay. About four miles long and 40 feet deep, Newport News is considered one of the finest natural harbors in the world. The city itself was settled between 1611 and 1621 by Irish colonists. In 1880 it became the terminus for the Chesapeake & Ohio Railway, and during the Civil War it commanded a view of the battle between the Monitor and the Merrimac.

It is there, on about half an acre of land that overlooks the James River, that Gladys and Alain Huyghe maintain their home and garden. From their terrace a visitor can look out over the water and watch the ships that come and go on their way either to far-off lands or local naval maneuvers.

The white stucco house with its roof of cedar shakes was designed by the Huyghes themselves. It has the romantic look of a house perched on the coast of Brittany some five thousand miles away across the Atlantic—both the Huyghes were born in France—but in this case the design is practical as well as picturesque. In this area hot and humid summer days often bring storms and the rains can be heavy. The Huyghes designed a center-canted, brick-paved strip that runs along the foundation of the house to lead away water from the gutterless roof. In front of the strip is a planting of Japanese holly

Left, the view from the road in front of the house, with a basket of colorful annuals.
Above, lobelia and wax begonias.

(*Ilex crenata*) that forms a background for the flowerbeds in the front yard. The area between the holly and the house also serves as a place to put pots of flowers that are not yet ready to be moved into the garden.

The front door is only 78 feet from the road, yet the distance seems much farther because of the shrubs and flowers that act as a buffer between the Huyghes' home and the world outside. A driveway of sand-colored, pebble-textured concrete runs diagonally across the front yard to the garage and is intersected by two paths.

"The first path," said Mrs. Huyghe, "is brick and runs up to the front door. The second is both a turnabout for the car and is paved to match the front driveway. After it crosses the main driveway, it changes to brick and narrows on its way to a corner patio. The angle where the two drives meet takes a bit of maneuvering for a car, but we originally did it to spare five one hundred and fifty-year-old red cedars (*Juniperus virginiana*) that originally grew in the front yard. In 1979, a freak tornado rampaged the neighborhood and took these and other trees with it. That wind smashed thirty of my containers. But it was a blessing in disguise because it opened up the

Early shasta daisies (*Chrysanthemum* 'May Queen') bloom in May along with an azalea, 'George Lindley Taber', and assorted annuals, bulbs, and perennials.

whole front yard to sunshine and now we have flowers."

The presence of neighboring houses on either side of the Huyghes is diminished by screens of evergreen shrubs including the beautiful heavenly bamboo (*Nandina domestica*), which brightens the winter scene with its red berries and bronze-toned leaves, and a little-known shrub, *Photinia × Fraseri*, a member of the rose family bearing small white flowers and glossy green leaves.

In May the path to the front door is graced by a large patch of the early-blooming shasta daisy (*Chrysanthemum Leucanthemum* 'May Queen'), a cultivar of the European ox-eye daisy that is hardy to Zone 3. To the left of the path is an azalea in a tub, *Rhododendron* 'George Lindley Taber', that contrasts brightly against the stucco of the house.

By July, from the road in the front of the house you can see the green domes of the holly, *Berberis* 'Crimson Pygmy', lilies, and a bright mix of annuals and perennials. On the side of the driveway nearest the street, a rustic basket holds pots of blooming marigolds in an eye-popping mix of orange and yellow, their color detracting attention from the now-browning leaves of the iris bed.

Behind the house a weathered brick terrace is home to a wealth of imaginative pots and antique garden furniture. It is narrow at one end and wider at the other and a low parapet that winds along the edge can be used as either a seat for viewing the river or as a place for more pots full of flowers.

There are amphoras and urns, jardinieres and old kitchen crocks, strawberry jars and odd clay vessels, Ali Baba jugs and pots with sculpted surfaces, all fascinating and all full of flowers. Brilliantly colored and healthy geraniums push their way over the edges of more cunning containers. An Italianate terra cotta pot holds a magic mix of *Rosa* 'Pillow Talk' and *Lobelia Erinus*—the colors striking when viewed through the open weaves of a white American iron-wire seat—only to be outdone by the contrast between a pink chaise lounge and a washed-gray wooden tub banded with strips of dark maroon that holds a bursting host of a *Hibiscus Moscheutos* hybrid.

"I dare not count all the containers," she said, "but I'm sure there are over one hundred of them. I use a basic planting mix of soil,

Opposite,
geraniums in
containers with a
view of the river
behind them.

peat moss, and vermiculite, usually cutting back on the peat moss for the geraniums. As far as the time it takes to water everything, I really don't know. I belong to my garden and never count the hours spent there."

Other containers on the terrace hold tropical plants that winter indoors including Madagascar jasmines (*Stephanotis floribunda*), and a shrub, yesterday-today-and-tomorrow (*Brunfelsia pauciflora* 'Floribunda'), with sweet-smelling flowers that bud and open to a rich, blue, turn pink with age, and eventually fade to white before passing from the scene. A half of an old wine barrel contains the golden-leaved *Berberis thunbergii* 'Aurea', quite striking when seen next to a drift of blooming blue flags and clouds of yellow *Aurinia saxatilis*. Mrs. Huyghe does all the work in the garden, except when there is heavy work like removing a tree.

And all of these chairs and pots are interchangeable, moved around at the owner's will on an imaginative chessboard in order to continually create a new combination and by so doing, a new picture. For this is first and foremost a garden of ideas, a garden filled with a bountiful variety of choice plants in stunning color blends, and obviously the home of an artist at work.

In addition to being a gardener, Mrs. Huyghe is a painter. "I've been gardening for over twenty years," she said, "and I see my garden as an extension of my studio.

"The season is about nine months of the year and I'm busy every moment of the day. My basic problem is that when I'm with the flowers I think of my paintings and the work I should be doing in the studio but when I'm painting I immediately think about the garden. I really need one to do the other."

The land falls off beyond the terrace, down to the James River and is carpeted with lilyturf (*Liriope muscari*) both for erosion control and ease of maintenance. Because of the USDA Zone 8 weather found in this region of Virginia, the plants are almost evergreen. Clumps of crape myrtle (*Lagerstroemia indica*) bloom in late summer. In addition there is a random planting of hollyhocks that gleam with reds, whites, and yellows, growing between the edge of the parapet and the slope below.

"When the crape myrtle bloom," she said, "they look like big vases of white and pink flowers set here and there along the bank. And I have planted many iris in between the liriope, choosing many different varieties so there is over a month of bloom."

In addition to the many flowers there are a number of blooming shrubs in the garden, including the bridal wreath (*Spiraea* × *Vanhouttei*), with its arching sprays of white, belying its reputation as an old American warhorse. And there are butterfly bushes (*Buddleia Davidii*) and tree peonies (*Paeonia suffruticosa*) with bold blossoms of white, pink, and red.

"There are several hundred plants in the garden," she said, "many purchased from local nurseries but many more raised from seed and propagated from cuttings. I often have a problem with where to put them. I had some clock vine (*Thunbergia alata*) and looked around for a place until I decided to let it twine up some fine thread I attached between the ground and an old lantern that hangs on an iron arm from an old post at the garden entrance. Eventually the vine looked like it was supporting itself."

When asked how she began as a gardener, she said: "When you have a house, first you fix the house and then you fix the garden. Flowers to me are as natural as having drapes in the windows."

"The only environment the artist needs," wrote William Faulkner, "is whatever peace, whatever solitude, and whatever pleasure he can get at not too high a cost." The Huyghes have found that environment.

A TENNESSEE GARDEN

THERE ARE TWENTY-FIVE towns and cities called Franklin in the United States. One of them is located in central Tennessee, about eighteen miles south of Nashville. This particular Franklin was settled before 1800, and became the scene of fierce fighting during the Civil War. Thomas Hart Benton, the American statesman—his grandnephew was the American painter—started his law practice in the town.

Virginia and Duncan Callicott have lived since 1966 in a house they built on a wooded knoll overlooking a view of rolling pasture, the Harpeth River bottom, and the distant hills of Tennessee, a scene that all in all resembles a Benton mural. Their home abuts a farm that has been owned by the Callicott family for thirty-one years.

"We built the house," said Mr. Callicott, "on a wooded ridge between two rolling pastures, right in the middle of a beautiful grove of elm trees, and the first garden became the floor of a natural cathedral, shaded by the gothic vaulting of the branches. But within three years the trees were lost to Dutch elm disease and we had to begin again."

Mr. Callicott was born in the Nashville area and although his parents were not gardeners, his great-grandmother once opened a flower shop and a cousin provided him with the first iris that started him on the road to horticulture. His brother farms the land and Mr. Callicott, a registered landscape architect, was for fourteen years the Executive Director of Cheekwood, the home of the Tennessee Bo-

Left, Mrs. Callicott weeds one of the borders in the front part of the garden. *Above, Tulipa* 'Jewel of Spring'.

tanical Gardens and Fine Arts Center. For the last four years he has been in private practice.

"One of the first garden influences in my life was reading *The Secret Garden*. I loved it. In fact I want nothing more than a square or rectangular plot surrounded by hedges; a secret garden in the Italian sense, just like the lemon gardens in Florence at Villa Capponi. Unfortunately, lemons aren't hardy in our Zone 6 climate."

"In my first garden," he said, "I had a wonderful crop of larkspur. A neighbor called my mother and wanted to cut them for Sunday church services. I made a policy on that day never to cut flowers in the garden again; they are to be enjoyed in the garden. I've relaxed a bit over the years and today when we need flowers for the table or for decoration, I have a crop of roses growing in an out-of-the-way spot to provide blossoms, and I'll cut peonies and daffodils."

The lawn is a freeform oval of green surrounded by exposed aggregate walks, a mowing strip of precast stepping stones. Edgings, according to Mr. Callicott, are the key to a neat-looking garden. Even if the plants are not always in perfect order, the well-groomed edgings give that effect. It's much the same as making a room look clean and neat by washing the windows and all the picture glass.

And that feeling of neatness even applies to autumn leaves. Since raking leaves is considered by the Callicotts to be a waste of time, the garden is oriented so that the prevailing winds blow the leaves off into the naturalistic borders of the garden.

The lawn is well-tended—the Callicotts believe that a lawn worth having is worth doing well so the area is small enough that it can be easily cared for. At the edge of the lawn is a raised mound shaped like a boomerang and measuring about 100 by 40 feet and about 4 1/2 feet high. It's a perfect and well-drained location for unusual plants, including small trees, perennials, and annuals, and makes an effective screen for the guest parking area. As to the lawn, Mr. Callicott advises that after the first frost, you lower the lawnmower blade to 1 inch, and continue to mow.

Clockwise from upper right, bottlebrush buckeye *(Aesculus parviflora)*, Japanese black pine *(Pinus thunbergii)*, azalea 'Treasure', dwarf variegated bamboo in a container, *Hemerocallis* 'Mary Todd', dwarf boxwood, and yellow coreopsis.

This results in the lawn becoming a soft brown carpet over the winter.

In early spring when the lawn has yet to green up, the first dots of color are the yellow tulips (*Tulipa* 'Jewel of Spring') that come into play after the forsythias (*Forsythia* 'Karl Sax') have finished blooming, and *Phlox subulata* creeps over the edge of the pathways. The tulip beds are replaced with orange impatiens for the summer months.

Looking out from the front door is a view of a burgeoning Japanese maple (*Acer palmatum* 'Dissectum') played against the pink blossoms of a Yoshino cherry (*Prunus* 'Yoshino'), a redbud cultivar (*Cercis canadensis* 'Forest Pansy'), a purple smoke tree (*Cotinus Coggygria* 'Royal Purple'), and various dogwoods (*Cornus florida*) including the pink-flowering 'Welch's Junior Miss', the white 'Springtime', the white 'Cherokee Princess', and the red 'Cherokee Prince'.

Under the maples are blooming snowflakes (*Leucojum vernum*), and the echoing mounds of flowers and foliage are seen against a striking black metal sculpture by Josh Green.

Later in the season a succession of bloom is provided by various azaleas, including a mixed lot of Exbury hybrids with yellows on one side of the yard and pinks on the other. These are followed by oakleaf hydrangea (*Hydrangea quercifolia*), pansies planted both directly in the border and in pots, and a profusion of the most American of plants, the

A view to the front of the house includes a threadleaf Japanese maple, *Hemerocallis* 'Raspberry Ice', and a rounded bun of holly (*Ilex helleri*).

daylily (*Hemerocallis* spp). The garden also contains hostas—the Callicotts have well over one hundred varieties—including the blue-green *Hosta Sieboldiana* 'Frances Williams' and the highly fragrant *H. plantaginea* 'Grandiflora'.

When plants have outlived their usefulness or grown too large for the scale of the garden, the Callicotts have the solution: "If it's in the wrong spot or outgrows its place, dig it up and move it somewhere else. If it's too big to move, cut it down." A continual reworking of garden themes has led to a number of discoveries: Clematis, for example, are planted at the base of trees and one hybrid (*Clematis* × *Jackmanii*) clambers up a crabapple, allowing the gardener to forget the bother of maintaining a trellis. When naturalizing daffodils, advise the Callicotts, use the old-fashioned varieties. Save the newer and jazzier varieties for a spot where the flowers can be cut for indoor bouquets.

Gardening is tuned to the cycle of the seasons: Everything old is new again. Mr. Callicott enjoys old gardening books and some years ago bought a copy of *Poetry of the Vegetable World*. He dipped into the book from time to time until one day it fell open to the second page. There was his great-great-grandfather's name. "One hundred years after my ancestor owned it, I bought it because of the title and the subject. Obviously I'm tuned to gardening."

IN THE GREAT SMOKY MOUNTAINS

ASHEVILLE IS IN THE western part of North Carolina and sits on the French Broad River, atop a plateau some two thousand feet high, surrounded by the Blue Ridge Mountains. The city was incorporated in 1797 and over the years has been closly identified with a number of American writers including O. Henry, who came there for rest cures, F. Scott and Zelda Fitzgerald (Zelda perished in a hospital fire there in 1948), and Thomas Wolfe, who was born in the city and lived in a boarding house known as Old Kentucky Home for the first sixteen years of his life.

The Great Smoky Mountains National Park, the Pisgah National Forest, and Mt. Mitchell—at 6,684 feet the highest peak east of the Mississippi River—are nearby and the state is home to nearly three thousand different species of flowering plants, over half of which thrive in the mountains around the city.

Just about five miles from the entrance to the well-known Biltmore Gardens of Asheville—an estate modeled after the great chateaux of France, built by George Washington Vanderbilt, and including a 250-acre parkland designed by Frederick Law Olmsted—lie the gardens of Doan Ogden.

The Ogden gardens were started in 1952. They are situated in the midst of the city, just a few blocks away from a major traffic artery, and lay protected from the surrounding world and its commerce, hidden in a wooded cove at the edge of a man-made lake called Lake Kenilworth.

Left, Lake Kenilworth is framed by the spring blooms of dogwoods and azaleas. *Above,* cottage pinks (*Dianthus plumarius*) bloom in the rockery.

Dr. Robert T. Kemp, Chairman of the University Botanical Gardens at Asheville, told me some of Mr. Ogden's history.

"Mr. Ogden's interest in botany," he said, "was somewhat accidental although he was always interested in nature and prefers to be called a naturalist. When he was a lad of ten, an elderly gentlemen in his neighborhood, one Emerson Price, introduced him to the world of plants. By the time he was nineteen he planned on going to college in Ohio, but a friend suggested that he become a landscape architect and attend Michigan State.

"He graduated in 1931, not exactly one of the better times to enter the job market with such a degree, and got a job with the church-supported Asheville Farm School (now Warren Wilson College) where local people could get an education in agriculture. In 1933 he met and married his wife, Rosemary, but times were hard and eventually he and his new wife went back to Michigan. They continued to visit the area on vacations. After Mr. Ogden served as a member of the 7th Army in Europe in the Second World War, they returned to Asheville and bought property on Lake Kenilworth."

The Ogdens' first home was a primitive one hundred and fifty-year-old log cabin from the Bent Creek area of the Blue Ridge Mountains. Originally a woodsman's cabin, it was taken apart and reassembled on their new land and was home for four years while they began to plan and lay out the gardens and build a new house.

The garden that surrounds the old cabin is planted with old-fashioned varieties of daylilies, perennial phlox, hostas, star-of-Bethlehem (*Ornithogalum umbellatum*), various primroses, snowdrops (*Galanthus nivalis*), and a number of jonquils (*Narcissus Jonquilla*).

Visitors enter the garden's nine-acre site through an azalea-lined drive which leads past a parking area, then winds between a moss garden and a stand of variegated bamboo (*Pseudosasa japonica variegata*), before reaching the Ogden house. Seven of the nine acres have been developed by Mr. Ogden into some twenty theme gardens, each individually designed to compliment the native flora of the area.

Each garden is designed for its own topographical niche and isolated from the others along the trail by the clever planting of trees and shrubs. As a result, visitors are continually confronted with new visual surprises as they stroll from one garden to the next. The entire site slopes gradually from above the lake, ending at a brook below a waterfall.

The mountains and wooded coves and valleys provide exceptional habitats for many plants that are usually found with a more northern distribution, plus sheltered spots for many plants that are not reliably hardy. This part of North Carolina is a fine place to garden. The climate is Zone 7 with the lowest winter temperatures usually between 5° and 10° F.

All told, there are about twelve hundred varieties of plants, including one hundred and fifty trees, three hundred and sixty-four shrubs, forty vines, ninety-four bulbs, two hundred and thirty-three perennials, forty-one ferns, and two hundred and seventy-seven wildflowers. Many are termed rare and unusual specimen plants.

The typed list of species fills twenty-three single-spaced pages.

The gardens contain many unusual plant combinations. The magnificent and rare dove tree (*Davidia involucrata*), a native of western China which bears flowers that look like white handkerchiefs waving in the wind, is found in company with the mimosa (*Albizia Julibrissen*). The Chinese tree of heaven (*Ailanthus altissima*) is only a few steps away from another Chinese export, the violet-flowered Princess tree (*Paulownia tomentosa*).

A walking tour of the gardens takes about one hour, and follows a winding trail that measures

Opposite, the faithful dog, Mo, patrols the rockery of the Ogden gardens.

three quarters of a mile. It begins at the Moss Garden and from there the trail leads to the Upper Gardens, around a garden pool, turns under an arbor, and then passes through a garden of hostas, down the steps of the Rockery, and onto the house lawn.

Spring blossoms grace the upper wall of the Horseshoe Garden.

The Moss Garden is based on the Japanese idea. It's a well-shaded area and is planted with native mosses gathered by Mr. Ogden over the years from the woods nearby.

From the front patio of the house there is a stunning view of Lake Kenilworth sparkling in the sunlight and framed in the spring by hundreds of dogwoods (*Cornus florida* and *C. florida* 'Rubra') and redbuds (*Cercis canadensis, C. canadensis* Forma *alba*, and *C. chinensis*) in bloom with the mountains behind.

After crossing the lawn, the trail descends through other theme gardens, eventually reaching a stand of hybrid rhododendrons and a grove of specimen trees. Then looping up through the Fern Garden one encounters the native rhododendrons of Jungle Trail No. 2, the Wildflower Trail No. 3, and the one hundred and eighty-year-old historic log cabin with its own garden, from which the steps ascend past the stand of bamboo and back to the parking area.

The Fern Garden alone contains over forty species of ferns, including both the evergreen and rattlesnake grape ferns (*Botrychium dissectum* and *B. virginianum*) and the Hartford or climbing fern (*Lygodium palmatum*).

The collection of wildflowers features both the American bugbane (*Cimicifuga americana*) and black cohosh (*C. racemosa*)—both deserving of a place in any perennial border—and the delightful Fraser's sedge (*Cymophyllus Fraseri*), which is often called *Carex*. This last plant belongs in every garden devoted to American flowers.

I asked whatever prompted Mr. Ogden to open his garden to the public.

"The amazing thing about him," said Dr. Kemp, "is his love of people. He's one of the few gardeners that I know who have encouraged the visits of children to the garden. And he has always used students from the college to help out with caretaking chores. In fact, the only professional help he ever had was to hire some earthmoving equipment for the original contouring of the grounds. In essence he always gave the same help to the children that he received when he was young."

One of the charming stories told about Mr. Ogden concerns his brother, who is a botanist. One afternoon the doorbell rang and the door was opened to reveal a group of fifteen gentlemen who were traveling by bus

to a horticultural convention. They told Mr. Ogden that they were fans of visiting arboretums and that his brother had told them to stop by and see the plants.

They were escorted through the gardens and just before they left, they brought out a potted plant and asked Mr. Ogden if he could identify it.

"Why, of course," he said, "I know what it is. It must be a Norfolk Island pine (*Araucaria heterophylla*)."

Later he confessed that he had never seen such a plant but thought that's about what it should look like.

As I write this particular interview, Mr. Ogden is very ill and the garden is—for the time being—closed to the public.

Thomas Wolfe is most famous for his novels that describe his life, including the years spent in Asheville. In *The Web and the Rock* he wrote: "If a man has talent and cannot use it, he has failed. If he has a talent and uses only half of it, he has partly failed. If he has a talent and learns somehow to use the whole of it, he has gloriously succeeded, and won a satisfaction and a triumph few men ever know."

Mr. Doan Ogden has succeeded.

A GARDEN OF ROSES

THERE ARE OVER one hundred and fifty entries devoted to the rose in *Bartlett's Familiar Quotations*. The beautiful lily boasts twenty-three, the daisy a mere fourteen, and the ubiquitous dandelion only three. The quotes run the gamut from Gertrude Stein's "Rose is a rose is a rose is a rose," (the correct count is four, not three), past the lines of John Boyle O'Reilly, "The red rose whispers of passion and the white rose breathes of love," up to this marvelous poem by Dorothy Parker:

Why is it no one ever sent me yet,
  One perfect limousine, do you suppose?
Ah, no, it's always just my luck to get
  One perfect rose.

The profusion of such rose references underscores the popularity of this flower throughout the world. And nowhere is the rose more beloved than in our own United States. After all, it's our national flower.

The gardens of Bruce Krasberg are chiefly devoted to the beautiful rose. His vast collection of flowers is found on a suburban street in Winnetka, Illinois, a city north of Chicago, on Lake Michigan, incorporated in 1869.

"I started to garden," said Mr. Krasberg, "with my mother, when I was a small boy, seventy-five years ago. For many years I did gardening chores for neighbors. Then I got married, had two daughters, built my first house in 1937, and at the age of thirty-one started serious garden-

Left, looking across the front yard with its island beds. *Above, Rosa* 'Electron'.

A view of Dr.
Krasberg's rock
garden.

ing with—upon the advice of a neighbor—a dozen rose bushes."

Serious does not adequately describe a man who at one time cultivated over seven hundred rose bushes and even now maintains over three hundred. His present house (a modified colonial of stone) sits on an acre of land surrounded by a clipped and vibrant green lawn, dotted with island beds of roses—including the front yard, since Mr. Krasberg believes that passersby would rather look at beds of blooming flowers than just shorn grass—that begin to bloom in early June and flower on until the first freeze.

"Roses," he said, "are to me the best all-around flowers in captivity. And even if you have only one perfect rose, it's still beautiful."

Mr. Krasberg's love of the rose and all things horticultural extends far beyond the borders of his backyard. He was a charter member and past president of the Men's Garden Club of Highland Park, a past national president of the Men's Garden Club of America, a board member of the Chicago Horticultural Society for the last thirty-four years, chairman of their Awards Committee for the last ten years, and was the first chairman of the prestigious Chicago Botanic Garden Committee. All this was in addition to being the President of the Krasberg Corporation, metal stampers and assemblers.

His regard for the rose has been pursued over the same span of years that saw the Chicago Botanic Garden turn a three hundred-acre tract of marshy forest preserve into the present gardens, where in 1985 opened a three-acre garden that represents the hundred rose varieties best suited for Chicago's climate. It is called the Bruce Krasberg Rose Garden in honor of his dedication to the design and placement of the garden and his help in the selection of the roses.

"Most rose gardens that I have visited in my travels," said Mr. Krasberg, "displayed the roses in oblong or parallel beds in stereotyped settings. While this makes for more convenient maintenance, I wanted something different and more interesting—a rose garden that not only dramatically showcased each class of roses, but did so in a more intimate manner..." The design succeeds by using a serpentine approach to the garden paths rather than the straight and narrow.

Back at home Mr. Krasberg's island beds also break the general rules of parallel bedding. "My wife and I," he said, "have visited seventy-two countries and we always go to see the rose gardens only to find them invariably planted in straight rows. So our approach was to mix the roses with other plants and plant them in groups so you could walk around the entire planting."

On the subject of the rose itself, Mr. Krasberg said:

"Starting with singles and doubles, there are many kinds of roses, but the basic rose that most people think of is the hybrid

Top, 'Betty Prior' is one of the oldest rose cultivars. Bottom, Rosa 'Chicago Peace'.

tea. That's the type found in most rose beds and producing the most spectacular blooms."

Other varieties found in American gardens include the floribunda (the result of crossing hybrid teas with polyanthas), which produce many flowers on a stem and are hardier than the hybrid teas; the grandifloras, a class that first appeared in mid-1950s and was established for the cultivar 'Queen Elizabeth'; climbing roses which can be trained to grow up a trellis or around and over an arbor; old garden roses, flowers that have been in cultivation since 1867; miniature roses, small enough to grow in 3-inch pots; species roses, those that occur naturally in the wild; and shrub roses, a group that includes the hybrid musk, the hybrid rugosa, and the polyanthas.

"The polyanthas," said Mr. Krasberg, "produce lots of blossoms and they last much longer than other roses—'China Doll' blooms will last for two weeks. Then," he adds, "there are the tree roses. They are spectacular but not very popular in this area because it's a real job to put them to bed for an Illinois winter."

The tree rose is a floribunda or hybrid tea that has been trained to branch out atop a straight 5- to 7-foot stem. They are very English and featured in Tenniel's illustrations for *Alice in Wonderland*, where Alice and the card family played croquet under their blossoms.

"Expect to pay from $11.00 to $15.00 for a good rose. Bargain roses are not a bargain in the long run; they are likely to be spent greenhouse stock that has produced flowers for sale and will now bear nothing but grief. But," he adds, "you can save a bit by buying plants whose patents have expired. The cultivar 'Peace', for example, is no longer under patent (they last for seventeen years, during which time the plant originator gets fifty cents back for each plant sold).

"It's important," said Mr. Krasberg, "that you have an idea of what kind of rose you want to buy and where you wish to plant it before you start. A diagram or layout of your projected garden is a big help. That way you will consider color, mass, and height requirements and how the rose might blend in with other plants in your garden."

Top, this large-flowered climbing rose, Dr. Nicholas, is a repeat bloomer. *Bottom,* a bed of roses surrounded by a white brick walk.

"Be very sure," he adds, "that you get three good stems, each about as thick as a man's middle finger—no bigger—on a good cane. And look very carefully for black spot, rust, or mildew. You can easily spot a healthy leaf."

When you shop for roses they are usually sold either packaged with bare roots or pot-ted up. Mr. Krasberg prefers to buy potted roses and gives three reasons for doing so:

"They are much easier to get started, you can obviously spot a bad bargain, and they can be planted out at almost any time during the season. Bare-rooted plants must be set out very early in the season, definitely not in the fall, because in the climate around Chicago they will surely winter-kill."

The most surprising thing about Mr. Krasberg's garden is his watering plan.

"It begins with fertilizing in the spring. I use a mixture of nitrogen, potassium, and phosphorus—it's what I use for the lawn—about a handful around each rose bush staying about 6 inches from the stem. Next I work the soil with a regular three-pronged hand cultivator, watching out for the roots, as they grow close to the surface. Then I give them a really good soaking. About three weeks later, I follow the same routine again, then after the soaking, I cover the beds with 3 inches of packed peat moss and never water again all summer long! Water can't penetrate the packed peat moss from above but it can't dry out from below. The peat moss provides insulation—on those hot summer days in the Midwest, the rose beds are always cool. I figure I use about twenty eight bales of peat every season."

"If you must water," he adds, "only do it if

there has been less than half an inch of rain during the week and then water in the morning: Roses should not go into the night with wet leaves because it promotes disease. It's always better to use a sprinkler or a soaker hose for three quarters of an hour in the morning."

Regarding fertilizing, Mr. Krasberg also advises that you never give roses nutrients after the middle of August because you want the plants to go dormant in the fall, not get high on plant food.

When it comes to picking roses for a weekend party or gathering, Mr. Krasberg has the following advice: "My wife and I start cutting on Wednesday or Thursday and go right through the beds and cut as many flowers as we think we'll need—I've been cutting the stems straight across ever since we started. We split the stems so they can soak up water and plunge them into a bucket filled with warm, not hot, water, letting them sit for a while. Then we put them into vases, cover them with plastic and store them in the refrigerator until ready for use."

In addition to one perfect rose, Mr. Krasberg lists among his favorites three double hybrid teas: 'Tropicana' (the first pure fluorescent orange rose, still the best in its color range, and the third largest seller in this century), 'Peace' (yellow edged with pink, and considered by many gardeners to be the rose of the century and the most popular hybrid tea of them all), and 'Paradise' (mauve petals edged with red and an All-America Rose Selection for 1979).

For winter, the roses are pruned to about a foot and a half from the ground and hilled up with some 10 inches of soil. Straw covers, advises Mr. Krasberg, invite rodents in to eat the plants and the styrofoam cones are more work than they are worth.

The rose garden then remains covered for the winter and in the words of George Cooper (who wrote *Sweet Genevieve*): "Hopeful hearts will find forever roses underneath the snow!"

A GARDEN RESTORATION IN CHICAGO

ON A MAP OF Illinois, the suburbs of Chicago ring the city in the same manner that the large "C" surrounds the "o" in the symbol used for American copyright notices. And no city is more American than Chicago.

The lands where the Chicago and the Des Plaines Rivers flow were walked in 1673 by Father Marquette and Louis Joliet. A trading post was established, and grew to an ill-conceived and poorly built city that became the scene of one of the great disasters of U.S. history when, in 1871, legend says that Mrs. O'Leary's cow kicked over the lantern that started the Great Chicago Fire. But the city grew again, and in 1933-34 it became the site of the Chicago world's fair, the Century of Progress Exposition.

In 1930, the landscape artist and designer,

Jens Jensen, designed a garden in one of those suburbs on a lot of approximately three and a half acres that included a ravine, a wooded area that he reforested with native plant material, and an area of 100 by 80 feet for flowers.

In 1978, Jo Ann and Stewart C. Nathan bought the house and the lot and Mrs. Nathan took on the job of restoring the garden.

"When I first started," Mrs. Nathan said, "I was so obsessed with the garden that I went out when the sun came up and stayed out until dark. My children learned how to cook when I was gardening. After all, Chicago weather is so changeable and the season is so short, you must take advantage of every good minute that nature provides. You have no choice."

Left, Jensen's original stone path winds its way along a border that includes daylilies, balloon flowers, phlox, and lilies. *Above,* blue and white balloon flowers (*Platycodon grandiflorus*) and *Phlox paniculata.*

The climate is Zone 5. Although there are winters when the temperature falls to -25°F, the garden is close enough to Lake Michigan that it benefits from a slight warming trend.

"When I became interested in Jensen," she said, "I began an adventure of research and discovery. Jensen was an American success story. Born in 1860, he emigrated from Denmark in 1884 and after traveling around the country—he worked for a short time on a celery farm in the South and doing odd jobs on a farm in Iowa—he and his wife settled in Chicago in 1886. Shortly thereafter, he found a job working for the Chicago West Park System doing menial tasks as a sweeper and general cleanup work in a potting shed.

"During that period, he and his wife took weekend trips on the trolley, rode to the end of the line, and from that point simply walked out into the open and unpopulated fields. There they would walk for miles and collect wildflowers. Rumor has it that the trolley conductors invariably gave them a hard time when they boarded for the return trip to the city, because they always looked so disheveled and unkempt."

Mr. Jensen started to develop such a love for the prairie and its flowers that he designed and planted a native wildflower garden in an empty spot of ground in Union Park. This was a prosperous part of town and all the local denizens were so impressed by the garden that his popularity grew and he began to rise in the park system. As the years passed he became the steward of larger parks until 1900, when—now with several children to support—he was fired from being Superintendent of Humbolt Park for not bending to the prevailing political system that was well-established in Chicago.

Without a job, Mr. Jensen turned to designing gardens, defining his theories of landscape design. Eventually he came to be regarded the dean of the prairie style of landscape architecture. He disapproved of the American passion for English and European plants and gardens, which caused gardeners to ignore the marvels found in their own backyards.

He began to champion native plants, particularly the plants that echoed the horizontal lines of the prairie. His favorites included native hawthorne trees (*Crataegus* spp.), redbuds (*Cercis canadensis*)—trees to 40 feet, known for their showy flowers early in the spring—and flowering crabs (*Malus* spp.). Mr. Jensen underplanted all these trees with groundcovers, and only later in his career did he turn to perennials. Unfortunately, he was largely ignored by the profession and

Top, a red hybrid tea rose 'Oklahoma' in the foreground and tuberous begonias in pots are backed by tall oaks and maples. *Bottom,* various daylily hybrids line one edge.

Another view of
the Jensen
restoration garden
with snow-in-
summer (*Cerastium
tomentosum*) tucked
into the iris leaves.

in 1935 he closed his office and retired to his summer home in Ellison Bay, Wisconsin. He died in 1951.

"The woods near the garden," said Mrs. Nathan, "were reforested with native trees, including hawthornes, sugar maples, and red maples. The original owner of the garden was from Alabama, and I still find plants that she must have wanted that simply hate this climate, including a wisteria that has never bloomed. The woody plants are basically those native to this area, while the herbaceaous plants range from native wildflowers to cultivated perennials and some annuals."

Mrs. Nathan spends fifty to seventy hours a week during the peak gardening seasons tending to the thousands of plants in the garden, although today she does have some help with maintenance.

"There are many wildflowers in the garden," she said. "White trilliums (*Trillium grandiflorum*), recurved trilliums (*T. recurvatum*), Virginia bluebells (*Mertensia virginica*), wild blue phlox (*Phlox divaricata*), hundreds of common violets (*Viola* spp.), squills (*Scilla siberica*), wood lilies (*Lilium philadelphicum*) and turk's-cap lilies (*L. superbum*), plus armloads of daylily cultivars (*Hemerocallis* spp.), hundreds of peonies (*Paeonia* spp.), and in the spring, daffodils by the hundreds. But there is still work to be done."

Sara Teasdale wrote: "Let it be forgotten, as a flower is forgotten..." Without Jo Ann Nathan, there would be one less remembrance of an American original.

A DESERT GARDEN IN THE MOUNTAINS

BOULDER, COLORADO, IS 5,700 feet up in the Rocky Mountains, twenty-five miles northwest of Denver. The city was laid out in 1859 and incorporated in 1871. Allan R. Taylor, Ph.D., is a Professor of Linguistics at the University of Colorado and a research associate at the Denver Botanic Gardens. He has been fascinated with plants since his teen years in the late 1940s, and has been desert gardening in Boulder since beginning his garden in 1972.

"Desert, or dryland, gardening," said Dr. Taylor, "is a natural choice for an arid or semiarid region. The issue is not so much the saving of water—though that was surely a major consideration in my case—but rather atmospheric humidity: Plants adapted to dry air do their best in dry air. Irrigation can supply moisture when needed by the roots, but supplying a moist atmosphere under an open sky is much more difficult. Then there is the aesthetic question: What better landscape can a gardener emulate than the regional landscape which surrounds his own garden?"

Dr. Taylor's interests were in the native vegetation of the West, and he combined them in a naturalistic planting using local plants and stone. His garden presently contains over one hundred and fifty plants, all acquired by collecting and by trading with friends who have similar interests. He grew many of the plants from seed. Although it began with an emphasis on cacti and other native succulents the garden now

---

Left, the garden in early summer. In the foreground is *Echinocereus reichenbachii,* and *Yucca glauca* blooms in the upper left. *Above, Echinocereus reichenbachii* in bloom.

includes perennial plants and shrubs from desert habitats.

"Successful dryland gardening in our area, where the precipitation is only about 15 inches annually [London, England enjoys 22.9 inches per year, New York City, a soggy 43, while New Orleans endures a wet 59 ¹/₂ inches], forces us to employ strategies in combating soil humidity, which in some parts of the year can be very high. Not only is there the problem of that concentrated moisture providing a hand for unwanted opportunistic weeds, there is also the possibility that so much moisture per year, particularly in the winter resting period, is far too much for some very desirable desert plants."

Desert or dryland gardening requires a discipline all its own. To begin with, the garden must be carefully laid out to provide both for almost total drainage of whatever moisture the clouds may provide and also for the evaporation of soil moisture. This can all be accomplished by a combination of the following three factors: exposure, incline, and soil structure.

Dr. Taylor defined each of the requirements: "My garden is 22 by 54 feet and located where other folks put the lawn. Ideal exposure is to the south or the west to provide the maximum sunshine and heat in all seasons of the year. Many desert plants require brilliant light and

On the left, front to back, are *Yucca harrimaniae*, the green-leaved *Arctostaphylos nevadensis*, and a shrub, *Cercocarpus intricatus*. The white flower spike belongs to *Yucca glauca*, and behind it is *Artemisia cana*.

Top, Penstemon crandallii blooms on the lower left, with Eriogonum corymbosum at center and Psilostrophe bakeri at upper right. Bottom, Opuntia macrorhiza.

considerable heat during their growing season if they are to be at all attractive to look at. In winter they need heat to melt away the snow as quickly as possible. But other exposures can work almost as well. My arid garden, for example, faces north. That was the only site available to me. But the less-than-desirable exposure can be compensated for in other ways."

Incline refers to the unevenness of the elevation. There is little room for a level surface in an arid garden—there are few such places in nature. "What we find," he said, "is a medley of slopes and inclines, all the ultimate response to erosion, elevation, and subsidence. By providing slopes and avoiding basins in the garden, we get rapid drainage and at the same time, create individual exposures within or microclimates for some plants that might find it impossible to survive in any other instance."

Finally there is the structure of the soil. The soil should be loose to a depth of at least 2 feet. This is usually accomplished by creating mounds of sand and fine gravel on the original surface. And it's a good idea to plow or otherwise work into the soil as much grit as possible before you begin to contour. The amount of sand and rock chips to be incorporated varies according to the nature of the original soil. A heavy clay, for example, requires a mix of at least 90 percent in sand or chips. Looser soils require less.

"Initial preparation," he said, "included contouring—I used spare soil from elsewhere on the property and plaster from remodeling of the house. There was a lot to dispose of and I thought it would increase the drainage by making the present soil loose and open. It turned out to be the right thing to do because the local soil is very alkaline and the calcium turned out to be quite beneficial. Most of the stone was hauled in from outside; I did have help with the large stones but

brought all the medium and small stones back in my station wagon."

After the garden site is prepared the next problem is what to plant. Although the best source of plants is direct collection from the wild, this is usually not a good practice since such collecting is often prohibited, especially on federal and state lands, and the plants usually do not transplant easily. Many states have strict laws regarding the collection of native plant material. But a number of small companies now exist whose owners have the permits and specialization needed to collect wild seed, and much good material can be obtained through them. Check your local botanic garden for information.

As far as what plants are best for such gardens, Dr. Taylor advises the following: "In large arid gardens, one or more trees add greatly to the natural appearance of the garden and provide good focal points. The best trees in the Boulder-Denver area are the pinyon or Mexican stone pines (*Pinus cembroides*), chiefly the varieties *edulis* and *monophylla* and of the junipers, I especially recommend *Juniperus osterosperna*, the cherrystone juniper (*J. monosperma*) and the very beautiful alligator juniper (*J. Deppeana*).

"Another conifer of great potential interest is the Arizona cypress (*Cupressus arizonica*). Though it's only thought to be hardy to Zone 6, some individual trees were known to survive -20°F

The garden in winter, with *Eleagnus commutata* at center left, *Yucca glauca* at center right, and *Opuntia imbricata* on the far right.

back in our winter of December, 1983."

Dr. Taylor also recommends a deciduous native, the desert willow (*Chilopsis linearis*); it grows best in Zone 8 but several survived along with the Arizona cypress. Other trees are the mesquite (*Prosopis juliflora* and the southwestern locust (*Robinia neomexicana*).

For shrubs he suggests the big sagebrush (*Artemisia tridentata*), which can reach a height of 7 feet in favorable conditions, and the fringed sage (*A. frigida*), native to the Colorado area and generally found all over the West, from the foothills to the high elevations. It is low-growing, intensely silver, and very downy in appearance.

Then there are the yuccas. They come in all sizes from tiny dwarf forms scarcely 5 inches in height to the giant Joshua tree (*Yucca brevifolia*) with stems reaching to 40 feet. All will bloom, when mature, with spikes of cream-colored bells which, if pollinated, produce fat ornamental pods. Only a few yuccas are hardy in the Denver area and these include the soapweed (*Y. elata*) and the popular banana or blue yucca (*Y. baccata*), with the variety *vespertina* giving the most striking steel blue color.

For beautiful flowers there are the many agaves (*Agave* spp.), the prickly pear cacti (*Opuntia* spp.), the barrel cacti (*Echinocereus*

Opuntia imbricata in bloom.

spp.), plus a host of other plants. High on Dr. Taylor's list are the California poppy (*Eschscholtzia californica*) — now available in many colors including white, pale yellow, and pink — lupines (*Lupinus* spp.), penstemons (*Penstemon* spp.), and the lily family, including both the mariposa lilies (*Calochortus* spp.) and the flowering onions (*Allium* spp.).

"The garden has been developing," said Dr. Taylor, "for thirteen years, with the last stones put into place in 1985. New plants are constantly being tried as the less appropriate choices die or are removed before they do. I expect that the garden will not reach equilibrium for several more years.

"And," he added, "gardeners should always remember that there are serious issues in a garden, since far more varieties of plants are combined there than would ordinarily appear on the same spot in nature. Nature rarely must accommodate a large number of disparate characters and she has but one way to correct our ill-advised planting decisions: she removes the plant. Gardeners should never forget that the thoughtlessly planted garden is a mere collection, a motley hodge–podge, possibly even a grotesque horror."

The carefully planted garden, however, can be a serene work of art and a complement to nature.

A HIGH DESERT GARDEN

ABOUT TWENTY-FIVE MILES north northeast of the city of Los Alamos, New Mexico lies the community of Espanola. Los Alamos was the site of an atomic bomb laboratory and in July, 1945, the first atomic bomb was tested on the Alamogordo Air Base in the southern part of the state.

The gardens of Nambé are the home of Dr. Robert Frasier. They are nestled on the western and dry side of the Sangre de Cristo Mountains, a part of the southern Rocky Mountains. At 6,700 feet, this is high desert country. The land overlooks the Rio Grande Valley to the west, where spectacular sunsets light up the volcanic Jemez Mountains, the ancestral home of the modern Pueblo Indian people.

Before the present Rocky Mountains rose upon the scene, an ancient volcano 28,000 feet tall exploded and changed the climate of the world. It was one of the largest explosions on Earth. Volcanic ash covered the ground as far as the Mississippi River and a huge caldera (the Spanish word for cauldron) was formed that is now filled with vegetation. The early civilizations in this area evolved around the volcanic warmth. In what must be one of the world's greatest ironies, the United States Government built the laboratories for the development of the bomb on the side of the Jemez crater.

"Evidence of man in this region goes back over twenty thousand years," said Dr. Frasier. "In the mountains nearby, there are caves that were occupied that long ago, cliff dwellings dug into thermally conductive volcanic stone—the winters here can plunge tem-

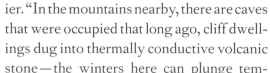

Left, the sunken garden with flagstone wall and serpentine retaining wall includes dwarf conifers, ornamental grasses, and dwarf blanket flowers (*Gaillardia* 'Goblin'). *Above,* purple iris against an adobe wall.

peratures to -32°F. And water is and has always been the limiting factor in life here in the Southwest. Centuries ago, the Pueblo Indians built irrigation pathways or *acequias,* to catch the snow melting in the spring to water their crops. And often modern man uses these same pathways, usually for the same reasons, and often for gardens."

The gardens form a rectangle of about 100 by 500 feet and are divided into five distinct areas which surround an old adobe home. The front garden is bordered by a long portal or porch, an area of lawn, and an acequia that supplies water to the community. This acequia is lined with stone, and large boulders covered with moss give it an ancient look. Three levels in the streambed provide both the lulling sound of water and mirrors to reflect the image of the garden. Dwarf conifers and various groundcovers provide color year-round.

"It was the house," he said, "that attracted me to the property. It's such a livable place and sits upon the land not as an intrusion but as an integral part of it. Old adobe houses are constructed so that every room connects to the outside. Early people would build the rooms, one after another, out of mud bricks and when they were finished, they would chisel an opening to connect them. Windows open to spectacular views of the sky and mountains so you literally live with the outside. Today the wisteria on the ramada is in full bloom and it is breathtaking."

The entrance area is a long drive that passes the wisteria-covered open ramada that connects the main house with the guest house. A xeriscape garden sits next to the adobe home and in addition to hosting a number of desert plants, provides support for the weakened walls of the building. A hedge of Russian olive (*Elaeagnus angustifolia*) acts as a long screen.

"It had to be a xeriscape garden in this spot," said Dr. Frasier. "If it were a garden needing regular amounts of water, the mud walls would be continually threatened. Only a dry garden would work here."

A private courtyard between the main and the guest house helps in providing a spot of coolness in the hot desert summer. The lawn—shaded by two elm trees—lies open to the west and focuses attention to the views of the old Nambé church and the mountains beyond. An acequia and a coyote fence borders on the west. This type of fence—made of whole cedar or juniper logs that stand on end—has been used for centuries by both the Indians and the Hispanics to surround and protect their homes and land. Properly made, such fences will last forever. The tops were set in an irregular pattern so that animals that did jump over were often caught in the small separations.

Behind the guest house is a wide expanse of lawn containing massive, old fruiting apricot trees. The trees are easily over one hundred years of age and have lasted far longer than most such trees in this part of the country. A developed acequia on the eastern side of the lawn follows the exact course of one used since the 1200s and enters a large irrigated basin. Water for the lawn comes from an electric pump connected to a well.

The use of such water has become a tangled legal problem. Private landowners are being sued by the Indians who claim that they own the mountain watershed and all the water that eventually reaches its way beneath private property. If you live in the area and own a well, the Indians wish to meter the water. The case is now before the New Mexico courts and will eventually go the Supreme Court. Since a great deal of private land now borders Indian land, it will be a major legal decision across the nation.

In this flood-irrigated basin area are three berms—narrow, level edges or shelves that extend from a bank or slope—and a sunken area that all function as dry islands. The rock berms echo the shape of the western mountains. They all contain moss-covered boulders and paths that

wind between both large and dwarf conifers, flowering crabs, plums, pears, hawthornes, and weeping cherries. The many weeping deciduous trees offer spring flowers and fall foliage, and their gnarled trunks and branches become winter silhouettes. There are some apple orchards in the area that are nearly three hundred years old and because the apples do well here, the crabapples and the *Malus* family in general are prosperous.

The sunken garden is an obliquely triangular area with a floor of dwarf pink dianthus (*Dianthus graniticus*), partially contained by a 44-foot-long serpentine, moss-rock wall in the shape of an *Avanyu*, the Pueblo Indian water serpent. This motif represents the Indian symbol for water and its resulting good fortune, and it appears on modern Pueblo black-on-black pottery in a stylized form. The final boundary of this bed is a slanted cambered retaining wall of boulders and red flagstone which absorbs and then reflects heat to help the weeping cherries through the cold weather of winter and early spring.

A dry stream bed of dwarf conifers, boulders, Siberian iris, and various groundcovers completes the irrigated basin area.

"Whenever I am traveling," Dr. Frasier said, "I look for conifers, groundcovers, and bring home various wild grasses to try. They are so beautiful in the sunlight that I wonder why more

The flood-irrigated basin area in spring with a white-blooming *Malus* 'Mary Potter' and at the right, *Yucca elata*. The pink flower is *Phlox subulata* 'Emerald Pink'.

people do not use them in gardens. Obviously, there are not enough grasses offered in the nursery trade."

The last garden is a productive fruit orchard with apples, cherries, plums, pears, nectarines, and peaches. Alpine conifers surround the orchard and act as a windbreak to modify the course of both winter and spring winds.

There are thousands of plants in the gardens and during the active months of the garden year, Dr. Frasier spends some thirty to forty hours a week outside. The only help he has is one man to share in the weeding chores. "I've done most of the work in making the garden alone," he said, "but I must acknowledge Mark Cherry for the rock work in the berms and walls."

"As to the plants," he said, "I love conifers both for year-round color and for the structure they provide, particularly in the winter. I don't use too many flowers in the garden. Flowers, I feel, are powerful expressions, especially if the colors are bright. I look for the blues in the conifers and, of course, the white flowering trees are grand. Trees and shrubs give the garden a permanent look while flowers, unless used with re-

Top, pink-flowered Brechtel's crab (*Malus ioensis* 'Plena') overhangs a berm planting of mugo pine, blue avena grass, *Iberis sempervivens* and *Tanacetum* spp.. *Bottom,* blue fescue grasses (*Festuca* spp.) overhang the acequia.

straint, result in an unkempt look.

"I recently returned from the Washington-Oregon and Colorado area with some new conifers for the garden, including the lace bark pine (*Pinus Bungeana*). This pine is often planted near Buddhist temples in China. It is slow-growing but spectacular when the bark peels in older specimens. I also brought back serviceberry or shadbush (*Amelanchier* spp.), an American tree that is well-known for both hardiness and colored foliage, and lovely bloom that comes before the end of April. I've had things in the ground for two or three years that I wish to change because the garden is never finished. And when I finish with medicine there is nothing that I'd rather do than landscaping for people."

After I talked with Dr. Frasier, I thought of a line from Willa Cather's novel, *Death Comes for the Archbishop:*

"In New Mexico, he always awoke a young man...He had noticed that this peculiar quality in the air of new countries vanished after they were tamed by man and made to bear harvests...that lightness, that dry aromatic odor...one could breathe that only on the bright edges of the world, on the great grass plains, or the sagebrush desert."

IN OLD SANTA FE

SANTE FE, NEW MEXICO was founded by the Spanish about 1609 on the ruins of an old Indian city. The city lies between the Pecos and the Rio Grande Rivers at an altitude of some seven thousand feet. It became the center of trade between the Spanish and the Indians for over two hundred years and it is the oldest capital city in the United States.

After Mexico gained its independence from Spain in 1821, the Sante Fe Trail became a trade route and the city became part of Mexico. In 1846, General S. W. Kearny and his troops took over and the region became a province of the United States. The Palace of the Governors is over three hundred years old and has been occupied by Spanish, Indian, Mexican, and American governors. New Mexico became our forty-seventh state in 1912.

Gladys and Julius Heldman moved to Sante Fe six years ago. Mrs. Heldman was the publisher, editor, and founder of *Tennis World Magazine*.

"It's an attractive and wonderful kind of living out here," said Mrs. Heldman, "with lots of snow in the winter, and summers with temperatures of 85° to 90° F but without any humidity. When we started the garden all we found were pieces of cement and rock. We had to do everything from scratch. We brought in 25-foot-high trees, including aspens (*Populus* spp.), and not one of them died.

"You can get hail in the middle of the summer here. It can knock down every flower and blossom. And this year, because

---

Left, dragon's blood sedum and red petunias 'Super Cascade' surround a mock orange bush in the courtyard. *Above*, torch lilies (*Tritoma* spp.) glow in the afternoon sun.

A Rio Grande salt cedar or tamarisk (*Tamarix ramosissima*) provides afternoon shade.

Valerians, marigold 'Inca', and blanketflower (*Gaillardia 'Goblin'*) blend with the adobe's color and texture.

of a late frost, our two huge, old apricot trees lost their blossoms and we won't get fruit this season."

The Heldman house requires a special kind of garden. Except for the windows, all the edges of the house are soft. It is a special triple adobe house designed by Carlos Vierra—he was considered the Godfather of the Sante Fe artists—and built between 1918 and 1922 as a showplace to arouse interest in a regional revival of the Spanish-Pueblo style of architecture.

"The adobe is marvelous," Mrs. Heldman said. "The bricks stay warm in the winter and cool in the summer. We have no air conditioner and the upkeep on the house is very low. Of course the enemy is water, but in this climate most of the precipitation is in the form of snow."

The Heldman's gardener, Emanuel Romero, is responsible for the flowers that bloom about the adobe house. The color combinations are in perfect harmony. Annuals in the form of petunias—he prefers the cascade type in purple, pink, and white—lobelias (*Lobelia Erinus* 'Blue Cascade'), and marigolds, in combination with perennial gaillardias (*Gaillardia × grandiflora* 'Goblin'), all are stunning against the purple-brown color of the house. And on the terrace, he has planted Harry Lauder walking sticks (*Corylus Avellana* 'Contorta') in pots, overwintering them in the garage.

"We built a little park," said Mrs. Heldman, "behind the garage using stone and sand. There is a grape arbor that holds five kinds of grapes, and you can walk through it. To save water we use a drip system, but unless you water artificially you cannot really garden here."

"We turn on the drip system in April," said Mr. Romero, "and turn it off at the end of October before the first freeze. It starts in the evening around six o'clock—the best time to water—and runs from fifteen minutes to an

A line of lobelia 'Blue Cascade' backed by various colors of pansies 'Pacific Giants' are in perfect balance with the adobe wall of the house.

hour. As long as the soil never dries out completely that's all the water you need."

Area gardeners can have a difficult time with most plants except for native trees and shrubs like the pinyon pine (*Pinus edulis*), junipers (*Juniperus osteosperma*), or the chamisa (*Atriplex canescens*)—which turns a beautiful sunshine yellow for three weeks in the fall but which, according to Mrs. Heldman, gives everybody hayfever.

Mr. Romero trims the chamisa and has used them for topiary. He cuts them with a pom-pom effect on the top of a full trunk. And, he adds, if you don't trim them they can be a fire hazard. His latest design for the garden includes planting ostrich ferns (*Matteuccia pensylvanica*) under the old-fashioned purple and white lilac trees that add a stunning accent to the house.

"For fruit trees," said Mrs. Heldman, "we have peaches, apricots, apples, pears, and cherries. They all do marvelously well in this climate. And our strawberries are the best in the world. It takes two years to get a good crop, then the third year they are great and just get better after that. We have three crops in the summer but since we're both allergic to them, we have a lot of friends during the strawberry season."

The colors of Sante Fe are desert colors: reds, browns, buffs, whites bleached by the sun, and a golden sun in a fierce sky of blue. Georgia O'Keeffe once said of her paintings of desert bones: "I have tried to paint the Bones and the Blue." Ms. O'Keeffe woulzd surely have approved of the Heldmans' house and garden.

A NATIVE CALIFORNIA XERISCAPE

REMEMBER WHEN THE SONS of the Pioneers sang: "All day we faced, the barren waste, without a taste of water—cool, clear, water?" You probably thought they were singing about time spent in Death Valley or the Great Salt Lake Desert. But the way things are going with water demands in semi-arid southern California, someday soon residents and owners of American gardens that happen to be way out West could well be singing that same song.

Water was once reasonably plentiful in Southern California. And whenever anyone needed more, wells were dug, aqueducts built, canals dredged, and about the only thought given to the future of water was as a plot device in movies

like *Chinatown*. Then came the drought of 1975-76 and the folks in northern California became nervous about their depleted reservoirs, and conservation became the byword.

In the October 5, 1986 issue of *The Los Angeles Times Magazine*, gardening editor Robert Smaus wrote: "With the exception of Santa Barbara, Southern California didn't suffer directly, but furious noises from the North, which relied on rainfall to fill its local reservoirs, forced us to join in the water-saving efforts. . . . Ten years have elapsed and gardens are as green as ever. But forecasting is a tricky business, and while our water empire is being expanded, it is ever under attack. Last year, burgeoning Arizona began

Left, part of the river of rocks in the Eliels' backyard. *Above, Kalanchoe* 'Fireball' in bloom.

Looking towards
the Eliels' house
from the Green Belt
across the street.

to claim its share of 'our' Colorado River water, and during the next few years it will take about sixty percent of what urban southern California now uses."

Alan and Lynda Eliel live in Laguna Beach. The town was incorporated in 1927, making it comparatively new as settlements go in the United States. It's primarily a residential community about fifty miles southeast of Los Angeles, thirty-five miles east of San Clemente Island, and located on the Gulf of Santa Catalina.

The Eliels worried about the luxury of using water for gardening and they were also concerned about conservation. So with the help of landscape architects Jana Ruzicka and Eric Katzmeir, they took an ordinary front yard and turned it into a xeriscape garden. Such a garden landscape is made of plants that need little or no water in addition to that provided by nature (the word *xeriscape* is a neologism created by the water department of Denver, using the Greek word *xero* for dry). In the Eliels' garden the xeric plants are thriving. And their front yard appears to be a natural extension of the land that is now a series of undeveloped lots across the street.

"The land on the other side," said Mr. Eliel, "is a native coastal chaparral known locally as the Laguna Greenbelt. We live so close to it that we decided that interfacing with a chaparral might not be a bad idea, and we created our garden to meld right into it. But creating a native plant garden in southern California is not that easy. Believe it or not, they are almost nonexistent here when they should, in fact, be the most predominant type of garden. We met a lot of resistance to our idea but the more other folks resisted, the more we persisted.

"Finally," added Mrs. Eliel, "we discovered the Tree of Life Native Plant Nursery in San Juan Capistrano. They had the plants we needed and that's when we really started to develop the plant theme and everything came together."

"The only sad thing about such gardens," said the Eliels, "is that here in Southern California

Various potted cacti and succulents line up in the front of the house like visitors from another world.

The silver-leafed Mexican rock daisy (*Perityle incana*), California poppies, sweet alyssum, and a prickly-pear cactus make an informal group.

they are few and far between. And even if you're not partial to flowers, the amount of indigenous bird life that is attracted to the native plants is far more than the number found in ordinary gardens."

Above and beyond the freedom from both growing and cutting the typical American lawn, there are three major reasons for developing a xeriscape. The first is the regional aesthetic that is the result of using plants native to the area; many of the lusher perennials popular in the United States strike a discordant note in the midst of sand, scrub, and stone. The second reason involves the conservation of water that results from such gardening, and the third is the amount of food that xeriscape plantings provide for the native birds. "The whole concept of such gardens provides a real ecological contribution," said Mr. Eliel, "especially when compared with the continuing overuse of conventional plant material in the majority of gardens in this area."

There are over three hundred plants in the garden and all of them came from local nurseries. Cacti overflow the edges of terra cotta pots, California lilacs (*Ceanothus* spp.) and California poppies (*Eschscholtzia californica*), Mexican purple sage (*Salvia leucantha*), and prickly pear cactus (*Opuntia* spp.), all bloom beginning in February (the Mediterranean climate of Southern California is not the same as the rest of the country). And the only use for the hose that lies curled up next to the Eliels' back porch is for washing the dog.

"We have a winter-wet and summer-dry climate," said Mr. Eliel. "The rains start in October and our plants are green all winter long, blooming to beat the band in spring, and falling back when the earth is dry and hot in the summer. It rarely goes below 40°F here along the beach, but ten miles inland the temperatures can occasionally go below freezing. The average yearly rainfall here is between 13 and 18 inches.

"In order to build the garden," he continued, "we removed all the grass in the front yard, three olive trees, and some shrubs. Next we tilled the soil with a rotary tiller, then the large boulders were brought in with a fork lift. The soil was mounded in some areas and more smaller rocks were moved in for the rock garden."

A fascinating feature of the garden is the stone rivers designed by Mr. Eliel and Mr. Katzmeir. They wind around and about the property, unifying the garden's overall design (see Paths and Paving, in Part Two, for a photo). Hundreds of boulders were moved by truck from a rock quarry in Palm Springs, and eventually formed serpentine curves of white, tumbling "water" that wind along between the house and the trees in the backyard.

It took about one week to build the stone rivers and the stone walls, involving 25,000 pounds of rock jockeyed into place by six workmen. The idea for the use of river rocks for making walkways and the dry rivers came from a team of late nineteenth century California architects, Greene & Greene, who were important in the arts and crafts style.

Shade is provided by native trees and shrubs which include the coast live-oak (*Quercus agrifolia*), a tree that eventually reaches 100 feet in height; the toyon, or Christmas berry (*Hetermeles arbutifolia*), eventually reaching 30 feet in height and native to the Santa Catalina and San Clemente Islands; the California bay tree (*Umbellularia californica*), a handsome tree that

Mexican purple sage (*Salvia leucantha*) and yellow ice plants *Mesembryan-themum* spp.), blue-eyed grass (*Sisyrinchium* spp.), and California poppies surround a group of rocks.

can reach 80 feet and is valued for its use in fine woodworking; the white alder (*Alnus rhombifolia*), another tree that can top 100 feet; the sycamore tree (*Platanus racemosa*), a 90-foot native found both in the area and south to Baja; the 35-foot California wax myrtle (*Myrica californica*), a tree especially well suited for growth in sandy and sterile soils; and the Parry manzanita (*Arctostaphylos Manzanita*), a shrub growing to 12 feet and bearing white or pink flowers with berries that are first white but change to red.

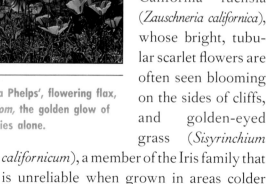

There are also a number of California redroots (*Ceanothus* spp.)—often called California lilacs—in the garden. These shrubs or small trees bear lovely blue flowers and are sun lovers. They should be grown in pots until moved to a final site, as they often resent transplanting. The carmel creeper (*C. griseus* var. *horizontalis*) is a fairly prostrate form, and other cultivars include 'Julia Phelps', 'Mountain Vision', and 'Concha'.

Top, a mix of Ceanothus *'Julia Phelps', flowering flax, and California poppies.* Bottom, *the golden glow of California poppies alone.*

The Eliels have about one hundred cacti and succulents in pots scattered about the porch and patio and their gardener, Michael Smith, is in charge of the watering details.

In one part of the front garden, clay containers hold various plants named for their resemblance to the animal world, including the beaver-tail cactus (*Opuntia basilaris*), the hedgehog cactus (*Echinocereus Engelmanii*), and the bunny-ear cactus (*Opuntia microdasys*), looking for all the world like interstellar visitors resting up from a long trip across the galaxy.

Among the California flowers found in the garden are the beautiful California tree or Matilija poppy (*Romneya Coulteri*), one species of a perennial herb that can reach 8 feet in height and which, when in full bloom, with white blossoms up to 6 inches wide, is truly spectacular. Unfortunately it is only marginally hardy to Zone 7 and often fails in colder areas, even with formidable protection.

Other denizens of the Eliels garden include woolly blue curls (*Trichostema lanatum*), a shrubby plant with purple flowers, California fuchsia (*Zauschneria californica*), whose bright, tubular scarlet flowers are often seen blooming on the sides of cliffs, and golden-eyed grass (*Sisyrinchium californicum*), a member of the Iris family that is unreliable when grown in areas colder than Zone 8.

In the spring the slope next to the house is alive with the silky tones of the California poppy, red flowering flax (*Linum grandiflorum*), and the blue of *Ceanothus* 'Julia Phelps'. If this is a sample of what can be produced with a minimum of water, there are a great many gardeners in the country who should replace topsoil with sand and gravel, stop paying their water bills, and try a new approach.

CALIFORNIA CACTUS GARDEN

PASCAL SAID: "ALL THE misfortunes of men arise from one thing only, that they are unable to stay quietly in one room." If that one room was in the home of Ruth Bancroft of Walnut Creek, California, and I could just occasionally leave to look over the collector's garden and then move on to the agave collection and the walnut trees, I know that I, for one, would be quiet for hours.

The city of Walnut Creek is in western California, east of Berkeley, and exactly ten miles from 4,100-foot-high Mt. Diablo. The town was incorporated in 1914 and for years was known for its production of poultry, fruit, and, of course, walnuts.

One hundred years ago, Hubert Howe Bancroft, historian, entrepreneur, and the grandfather of Ruth Bancroft's late husband, established his home and a large collection of walnut trees in what was then a peaceful valley. He had arrived in 1852 at the gates of San Francisco with $5000 worth of books and soon became the owner of the largest book and stationery business west of Chicago.

Unfortunately, as Walnut Creek expanded the groves of magnificent trees were cut to make way for tract housing and the Bancroft estate slowly shrank to its present twelve acres.

Mrs. Bancroft has always been a collector, only she set her sights on plants instead of china or paintings and kept them under wraps. The garden that existed at that point was merely one that looked like everyone's idea of what a garden should be.

In 1971, as the last two acres of walnuts

Left, looking across the field of agaves toward the shade house in Ruth Bancroft's garden. *Above,* opuntia and daisy-like lampranthus flowers.

Agaves abound in this garden. On the left, a century plant pushes its huge flower spike skyward.

This slope contains *Euphorbia Wulfenii* with its yellow-green flowers, the bright white blossoms of *Spiraea cantonensis*, a tamarisk tree on the left, and a blue wisteria at the top of the hill. Directly behind the euphorbia is *Viburnum Burkwoodii*, and to its right, *Phorium tenax.*

had declined, Mr. Bancroft suggested to his wife that she bring some of the plants that she kept in a series of lath houses, glasshouses, and garden frames out to the open air and start a garden.

So Mrs. Bancroft emptied the rambling structures of their inhabitants and unleashed a mob of cacti, aloes, agaves, and echeverias, along with hundreds of their succulent brethren, out upon the fledgling landscape. Most were *xerophytes* (the Greek word for dry plants) and looked more like a gathering of Steven Spielberg creatures than a collection of flora. Their plump, puffy, rounded leaves are coated with wax to prevent water loss and lend the plants a slightly cherubic look that is soon belied by contact with their prickles and thorns, armaments perfectly adapted to warding off desert marauders in search of any water they can find.

"I had Lester Hawkins do the initial layout for the raised beds," said Mrs. Bancroft. The late Mr. Hawkins was the co-owner of Western Hills Nursery of Occidental, California, and in addition to being an honored nurseryman, photographer, and garden writer, was himself an arch collector of plants from the drier parts of the world, including much of Australia and South Africa. "The beds were made up of compost, soil, and humus," she added, "mixed and hauled into the garden; included in the mix was all the soil from the pool excavation."

Since the climate of Walnut Creek is hot and dry for the summer months but reasonably cold in winter—temperatures can and do fall below freezing—and often wet with rains that persist for days, the plants need the perfect drainage that the beds provide.

Because many of the plants find water anathema, they must have protection from the rains of winter. "I have about three hundred frames of wood," she said, "and polyethylene. In size, they range from a cubic foot to 20 cubic feet. They take anywhere from three to four

Looking through the Alhambra-like arches of the shade house at a bed of agaves in bloom with 35-foot flower spikes reaching to the sky. Palo verde and other trees provide a soft background.

weeks to put in place and stay there from October into April.

"Right now," said Mrs. Bancroft, "I have one permanent helper for the heavy work and I couldn't get along without him. I start every day at 8:00 in the morning and go on until dark. I usually don't stop to eat lunch."

The plantings were mapped as islands surrounded by streams of winding gravel paths, so as the visitor walks the grounds, a new discovery is evident after every turn along the way.

Close to the house—a beautiful home of gray stucco with a gabled roof and windows guarded by slatted shutters of olive green—the garden plan remains somewhat traditional, but it, too, has its surprises: There is a large oval lawn that is surrounded by perennial beds and off to one side a rose bed of various single- and double-flowered species. The rose bed soon joins a

border of bearded iris that contains hundreds of cultivars, blooming as only they can when luxuriating in the California spring.

    The exotic look of the more traditional part of the garden is best typified by the beds of white calla lilies (*Zantedeschia* spp.) that grow in almost rank profusion, sharing space with a grove of pink flowering maple (*Abutilon* 'Apricot Bells'), and all in the shade of a free-blooming bower of Chinese wisteria (*Wisteria sinensis*). The total profusion of flowers is such that the bees from the surrounding hillsides find it difficult to choose a direction, much less tell others about the garden when they do their compass dance back at the hive.

    As one leaves the confines of the house, the more adventurous part of the plan surfaces, the clipped green grass gives way to the open landscape of the desert, and the garden

A luxuriant grouping of white calla lilies, blue wisteria, and flowering maple.

becomes truly American.

There are many opuntias (*Opuntia* spp.), a common cactus with deceptively soft-looking pads equipped with patterned rows of tiny but infectious spines, in Mrs. Bancroft's collection. These plants share the artificial desert with blooming banks of lampranthus (*Lampranthus* spp.), their succulent leaves hidden by hundreds of orange and yellow daisies, all in sharp contrast to the ruby red fruits of the cactus.

Agaves abound: *Agave Franzosinii*, a large member of the century plant clan, has silver-white leaves that act as photo negatives. As they open to the sun, each bears the unmistakable imprints of the previous leaf that covered it. A cultivar called 'Variegata' has leaves of dark green edged with wide stripes of yellow, only this plant chooses to wave and bend its leaves rather than stand sentinel-straight. Finally, there is the smaller and silver-leaved *A. parryi*, a native of Arizona that grows in the partial shade of a beautiful flowering palo verde, *Parkinsonia aculeata*.

One of the most striking color combinations in the garden combines the blue-gray of the sisal hemp (*Agave sisalana*) with golden yellow blossoms of a senna bush (*Cassia cremophila*), the flashy Hollywood relative of the partridge pea (*C. fasciculata*) that grows in sandy soil in the Northeast.

In late afternoon in the shade house, the visitor looks through the Alhambra-like arches to see the agaves to the left and the pool beyond, its surface covered with white water lilies. Beyond the shorter flower spikes of the blooming *Agave Victoriae-reginae*—named in the Queen's honor but at home in Coahuila, Mexico—reach a height of 4 feet. But they are dwarfed by the floral spikes of the neighboring *A. Franzosinii* that shoot 35 feet into the sky.

"It doesn't take a century," said Mrs. Bancroft. "They really bloom after ten to fifteen years. But it is true that they put so much effort into one of those fits of blooming that they simply fall back and perish. And unfortunately most do not produce enough suckers to carry on a display.

"The pool was Lester's idea," she added, "but I like it. He made the original plan but I planned the plantings because I wanted the fun of doing it."

And it's obvious from seeing her garden that Mrs. Bancroft has had a world of fun.

Top, a striped *Agave picta,* left, and *Aloe* × *spinosissima* in bloom. *Bottom,* the blue-gray leaves of sisal hemp contrast beautifully with the golden blossoms of a senna bush.

AN ARTIST'S HILLSIDE GARDEN

THERE ARE SOME GARDENS so alive with color that a first confrontation shocks the eye and stops it cold. There are others so endowed with textures—be they rock, wood, leaf or lichen, hard edges or soft petals—that their surfaces call out for touching in the same manner that successful sculpture must have its outlines traced by the human hand. The gardens of Harland Hand have both color and texture.

The gardens cover a little over half an acre of sloping land in the city of El Cerrito, California (incorporated in 1917). Shaped roughly like a triangle 274 feet long and 85 feet wide near the base, the house sits at the apex and looks out over the eastern shore of San Francisco Bay. The spaces within the triangle are divided into what Mr. Hand calls shelters, rooms without walls, rooms with a ceiling of sky, rooms where that sky becomes a special part of the composition, all made in the image of the spectacular and fissured landscape of the Sierra Mountains.

"I have found," he said, "certain places in nature where I could stop and be sheltered from the wind. These places have inspired the rooms."

About one hundred fifty miles inland, just south of Lake Tahoe and around Silver Lake, near Carson Pass in the Sierra Nevada, Mr. Hand found the natural vision that he wished to

Left, looking toward the house. In the foreground is *Bergenia* 'Silver Light'. The spiky plant halfway up the hill is *Phormium tenax* 'Variegatum'. The orange flowers belong to *Aloe* hybrids. *Above,* red-flowered *Crassula falcata* grows near a tree fern.

reproduce around his home. But once back in California, he realized that the rocks on his hillside were mere pebbles compared to the master stone of the mountains, for all he owned was a thin layer of soil that covered a sandstone ridge. With the eye of an artist, he saw the solution and proceeded to construct his own rocks. But instead of using molten lava in an imitation of nature's million-year-old, pale gray hunks of granite, he poured some 200 cubic yards of concrete made with a mix of five parts of sand to one part of cement. The liquid mash metamorphosed into fifteen seats and ledges, a cliff some 60 feet wide and up to 12 feet high, nineteen pools, and over two hundred boulder-like steps.

"I call the form sculptured concrete," he said. "And I did not use any aggregates in the mix because the pebbles would have made sculpting quite difficult."

In the early stages a bulldozer was brought in to do the heavy work of shaping the cliff, but once that was done, all the other work has been done by Mr. Hand.

The various levels of the garden were gauged by eye: no plumb lines or forms or molds were used. The surface textures are the result of sprinkling the wet concrete surfaces with an uneven coat of dry cement and smoothing it to an irregular shininess.

Paved areas of the garden are furnished with benches of concrete with "throw pillows" made of echeverias and armrests of gnarled rosemary.

"I have not made imitation rocks," he said. "I have made concrete do what I would like rocks to do. I chose concrete because I could maneuver it into the rounded, irregular flowing forms that I had seen in the Sierra. And it is only because of the beneficent climate of this part of California that I have succeeded. Without the curse of frost I never had to worry about heaving and cracking of the concrete."

Although the temperature is kind, the

In spring, rhododendrons bloom behind a concrete divider.

Pools fill basins sculpted from concrete by Mr. Hand. Silvery *Stachys byzantina*, *Festuca ovina* 'Glauca', and tree fern grow along the steps.

summers are very dry around San Francisco and Mr. Hand's garden is dependent upon an artificial circulatory system of underground plastic arteries. They eventually end in 10- to 15-foot high pipes topped with sprinkler heads that produce rain every five to seven days, depending on the time of year.

Mr. Hand was born in Minnesota and his first garden was started at the age of five when he experimented with a few radishes and some annuals. He soon graduated to a rock garden planted with wildflowers, and in 1934 won a Minnesota State Walgreen gold medal for a hillside rock garden with flagstone paths and ponds.

He moved to California in 1948 and graduated in 1952 from the University of California at Berkeley with an M.A. in Art, majoring in sculpture and painting. He went on to teach biology and physiology in high school and painting to adults. In 1978, Mr. Hand was given the Man of the Year Award by the California Garden Clubs.

"We have just begun to develop garden design in California and the West," he said. "The possibilities seem limitless. My designs are based on the nature I have seen in the mountains, on the gray granite glacial washes. I like to use unusual plants in unusual—but natural—ways. This, after all, is what nature does. And I go to those mountains, the seashore, the desert, meadows, and even to the microscope for inspiration. We have to develop the garden as art."

Adding to the
garden's beauty is
its marvelous view

For those gardeners who wonder how much time is devoted to Mr. Hand's garden, he said: "I generally work alone throughout the year, averaging about six hours a week in the garden."

Have you ever noticed the brightness of an orange candy wrapper stuck to a wet and glistening sidewalk on a rainy day in the city? Or the brilliance of the maple leaves falling across the late gray autumn sky? "Thy woods," wrote Edna St. Vincent Millay, ". . .all but cry with color." Because the framework of Mr. Hand's garden is gray, the orange blossoms of the aloe hybrids, the pink of a flowering maple (*Abutilon* spp.), the yellow of a sweeping mass of *Gazania uniflora*, or the bright red flowers of *Crassula falcata* pop like that tiny dot of red always found in a Corot painting. Gray is neutral; it lacks all color. Thus the intensity and hue of true colors are enhanced when viewed against a background of gray; flowers become the unfurled umbrellas of the city.

In most of the shelters that are found in life, the furnishings are decidedly non-organic. In one of Mr. Hand's shelters the following plants are the carpets, curtains, wall hangings, and floral bouquets: *Iberis sempervirens* makes a white mound between the concrete tiled floor and next to it a white rose (*Rosa* 'White Masterpiece') echoes the white of blooming calla lilies (*Zantedeschia* spp.), which in turn are shaded by a clipped Japanese wisteria (*Wisteria floribunda* 'Longissima Alba'). Opposite the wisteria are the lacy and light green fronds of an Australian tree fern (*Alsophila* spp.) and toward the back of the room are more calla lilies, these gracefully arching over one of the garden's many reflecting pools, a pool that contains pots of white waterlilies (*Nymphaea* × *virginalis*), while set into an imagined wall at the far end of the room, a *Leptospermum* 'Ruby Glow' becomes a three-dimensional stained glass window made of hundreds of deep red and glowing shards.

The pools, by the way, vary in size from 14 feet across to a mere 36 inches and in this case were made of a mix of four parts of sand to one of cement, each given additional strength by reinforcing rods, wire fencing, or chicken wire (depending on the size of the pool), sandwiched in 4 inches of the concrete.

In another area of the garden, Mr. Hand combined a lily-of-the-Nile (*Agapanthus* × *hybridus*), white cymbidium orchids (*Cymbidium* × *hybridus*), hardy geraniums (*Geranium* spp.), a tree fern, and a camellia (*Camellia* spp.).

And in what is one of the most inspired combinations, a living stream of *Echeveria elegans* churns over and around the river's rock bottom, while the river's edge is shaded by a grove of coral aloe hybrids (*Aloe striata*).

About his approach to planting, Mr. Hand says: "First the plant must survive where I put it and second, it must be artistic."

As to a philosophy of gardening, Mr. Hand says: "There are three main things in nature that can be used to capture certain moods within a garden. The first is the trail that gives you a sense of place, of someone having been there before. The second is a lookout, a vantage point, a view—it has a great sense of power and is quite primitive, revolving around food, animals, danger, and survival. The third is shelter, the place that gives you a sense of peace. That's what my garden is all about."

FOUNTAINS IN A CITY GARDEN

WHEN e. e. cummings (himself an American original) wrote: ". . .among the slow deep trees perpetual of sleep some silver-fingered fountain steals the world," he might have been describing another uniquely American garden, the backyard of Tom and Carla Fawcett's San Francisco townhouse, a place where the greenery of the garden definitely takes second place to the tumbling waters of two fountains that just might steal the show.

The new garden began when their next door neighbor inadvertently cut the roots of the ivy that created a 20-foot-long privacy hedge between the two properties. When the ivy died it left behind nothing except a tattered fence, not exactly the best view when settling down for a quiet and tranquil evening in the backyard.

Such small vicissitudes often lead us on to new and better things, and in this case the Fawcetts attempted to find something, perhaps a fountain—anything to detract attention from the fence.

They considered and dismissed stone putti; rejected gnomes and their animal cousins, the lions, tigers, and bears; and vetoed any use of squat Thinkers or midget Davids—the kind of concrete kitsch that often passes for garden art. Instead they approached an old friend, Aristides Demetrios, a sculptor who had recently completed work at the Monterey Bay Aquarium, where his high bronze fountain, aptly called *Forms Sung in a Kelp Forest*, was installed.

Left, looking toward the second-story deck. The stream in the center of the photo is edged with horsetails. *Above*, cymbidium orchids.

Then the Fawcetts asked landscape architect Richard Schadt to design the proper background for the fountain that Demetrios created.

"I've always been fond of sculpture in a garden," said Mr. Schadt, "so I suggested that instead of one fountain, they consider two and immediately placed the first—called the small fountain—in the center of the yard rather than against the fence. Then the sculptor was asked to work out another, larger concept. He did so and quickly moved from table-top models to life-size replicas made of cardboard planes supported on a finished armature—it resembles a mass of coat hangers found abandoned in a closet—that contained the plumbing. Water flow and resultant reflections were now considered, then the cardboard pieces were used to create templates for the bronze sheet-metal that was welded to the form."

The fountains are now the unifying factor in the garden. The pleasant burbles of falling water combine with the splashes produced when the water strikes the stream that curves between massive boulders, to effectively mask out many of the unwanted background noises of a city. If you step out from the breakfast room to the second-story deck, only the tip of the 15-foot-tall fountain is visible. By descending to a lookout landing you can view the entire 32- by 60-foot garden. The garden now consists of a brick patio and the stream (with its headwaters at the base of the large fountain) that meanders under a bridge, divides the stone paving of the yard and ends with the smaller fountain. To the right of the garden is a spa tub, now shaded by an open trellis that extends to the left of the deck, completing a visual triangle with the fountains.

"That trellis," said Mr. Schadt, "was the only thing the Fawcetts and I ever disagreed about. Mr. Fawcett thought it would conflict with the open feeling he wished to project. But after it was completed, they saw how it was just another visual link in the composition."

I asked him to describe the colors of the two fountains.

"The larger fountain is bronze," he said. "Natural bronze has a kind of a gold color and

The upstairs deck with its many potted plants.

The large bronze fountain, golden in color.

The smaller fountain with its blue-green patina.

weathered bronze has a patina of green, but this turned out to be a combination of browns and deep golds without any hint of green at all. The smaller fountain has a blue-green patina reminiscent of lichen-covered rocks.

"Bunches of fortnight lily (*Dietes vegeta*) and horsetail (*Equisetum hyemale*) grow between the stones at the water's edge. Between the rest of the stone paving we planted isotoma (*Laurentia* spp.), but it isn't too happy with the shade so we might change that to Irish moss (*Selaginella Kraussiana*)."

At ground level the brick patio is surrounded on three sides by wide planting beds. "A few plants from the original garden still remain," said Mr. Schadt. "They lend a feeling of maturity to the garden. A purple-leaf plum tree (*Prunus* 'Pissardii') provides the basic canopy of foliage and provides continuity with neighboring yards and gardens. The other permanent plants include a clump of paper birch (*Betula papyrifera*), a Japanese maple, rhododendrons and azaleas, a spattering of ferns, some species of viburnum, and the beautiful heavenly bamboo (*Nandina domestica*). [Heavenly bamboo is not a bamboo at all, but a member of the barberry family and unfortunately it is reliably hardy only to Zone 7.] Bougainvillea, jasmine, and wisteria have been encouraged to climb the trellis."

The Fawcetts admit lacking green thumbs but they stock various planters about the yard with pastel pink petunias during the summer months and daffodils in spring. The upper deck has many potted plants, including ivy (*Hedera helix* 'Hahn's Self-branching'), and long sprays of cymbidium orchids — quite happy in San Francisco's chilly nights — that add a distinctly tropic air. Various other potted plants that the Fawcetts happen to find in their travels about the city also show up in the garden.

"It is now," said Mr. Schadt, "one of the nicest city gardens I have worked on."

THE RARE AND THE COMMONPLACE

IN 1959 LESTER HAWKINS and Marshall Olbrich left their San Francisco apartment after buying three acres of wild land in Occidental, California—a very small town ("two blocks long and three restaurants," said Mr. Olbrich) about 60 miles north of San Francisco. "There followed," he said, "heroic years of ditching and mounding, pulling out blackberries and poison oak, and the periodic scraping up of money to sustain us."

Around 1973, Mr. Hawkins—who had been planning private gardens for a living—began designing and then supervised the installation of large-scale plantings for both condominium and apartment complexes. These activities subsidized their garden and their small and distinctive nursery, called Western Hills.

"We stock a wide range of perennial plants," said Mr. Olbrich, "and do most of the propagating ourselves and of course, it's a seven-day-a-week job running the nursery. It was started, by the way, to support the garden."

Mr. Hawkins was a natural gardener in two senses of the word. When working with plants he was a natural; the knack seemed to be in his genetic code. And he also believed strongly in the natural order of the garden. He disapproved of the stilted artificiality that brings to mind a garden where dwarf conifers resembling rounded buns encircle a geometrically patterned sprawl of tropical bedders and elegant jardinieres holding masses of impatiens and red geraniums. His garden would never have a per-

Left, a bridge over a tiny stream is half-hidden by shrubbery. *Above*, *Miscanthus* sp. (right) and giant reed, *Arundo Donax* (left).

fectly round ornamental pond where the first leaf to fall on the water's surface would be quickly (and quietly) whisked away.

By the late 1970s, Mr. Hawkins had traveled widely and engaged in plant photography. He also wrote many essays for *Pacific Horticulture*.

In an article on the plantsman's garden he wrote extensively of his philosophy: ". . . densely planted borders, vine on pergolas and walls (and sometimes on trees and shrubs as well), rock and dry wall gardens chock full of plants that thrive there, ponds edged with reeds, water irises, cannas, and much more. As we walk into the woods, the paths are bordered at first with closely planted sun-loving plants, then those that like the shelter and frost protection of dappled shade, and finally the genuine shade lovers."

On the subject of mixed plantings, he wrote: "Perhaps the most useful planting for small gardens and one that can be extraordinarily handsome almost anywhere is a border that mixes, more or less deliberately, the basic categories of plants—basic, that is, in the gardening sense. Perennials, shrubs, bulbs, and grasses can be combined in ways reminiscent of memorable scenes in nature and capable of providing interest the year round. I remember in Greece in late spring, on the island of Evia, a mixture that could well be copied just as it was. In the middle ground were euphorbias, lavenders, and campanulas (some of which were twining through the lavenders). These were backed by brooms and rock roses with low meadow annuals and bulbs—mostly anemones—in the foreground. For a garden we might want to extend the flowering season by adding later-flowering bulbs—*Allium christophii* (*A. albopilosum*) and *A. pulchellum*, perhaps—and some summer- and fall-flowering low perennials—origanums undoubtedly, and helichrysums. . .

"Innumerable plants are available for the mixed border, but it is important to keep them all more or less within the same general scale (a useful cue one can take from nature) . . . .

"A mullein, for example, may shoot skyward out of a bed of thistles by the roadside. The mullein has larger leaves, greater height, and a thicker stem than the thistle, but both are lowland plants, and neither looks out of scale. If. . .we [plant] a diminutive dianthus with artemisias and

Siberian wallflowers in the foreground harmonize with a drift of soft blue forget-me-nots.

lavenders a foot or more high . . . [the dianthus] will look out of place from the start.

"The mixed planting is ideal for displaying plant collections, provided the plants are of a size to be accommodated. A collection of dwarf grasses or sempervivums, for example, can be planted along a curving path together with bulbs, small perennials, and alpines of the right size in a way that gives a natural touch without detracting from the enthusiast's interest in the plants themselves."

Mr. Hawkins' own garden is a careful blend of the rare and the commonplace: ornamental grasses bend to touch a shaded path, itself bordered by drifts of wildflowers. The garden pool is not round but a clever linking of three circles, each overlapped, and the resident waterlilies share space with the aforementioned falling leaves. A bridge over a tiny stream is half-hidden by the shrubbery; a bench resides in the shade of a wild bower.

Today Mr. Olbrich operates the nursery and maintains the garden. "The average temperature here in the winter," he said, "is about 25°F, with 60 inches of rain during the winter and mostly drought for the summer months. Luckily we have a good well in order to water the garden."

In the summer of 1984, during a visit of Beth Chatto, English plantsman and garden writer, Mr. Hawkins said: "The plants have been good to us."

"And indeed they had," said Mr. Olbrich. "We had an agreeable way of making a modest income, a garden that was a refuge in what seemed an increasingly perilous world, and, above all, through plants we gained many valued friends, who gave Lester affection in his health and sustained him through his illness."

Mr. Hawkins died on January, 22, 1985.

RHODODENDRONS IN THE NORTHWEST

JUST ABOUT SEVEN MILES due south of Portland, Oregon, lies the city of Lake Oswego. Next to a narrow lake, the town was founded around 1850, incorporated in 1909, and is close to French Prairie (the French were the original settlers hereabouts) where an actual rodeo is one of the highlights every year.

The area here is very bucolic. After passing a working dairy with a number of cows chewing in a nearby pasture, you continue along a steep and very winding road until suddenly you confront a fairyland mix of colors that announces your arrival at the gardens of Cecil and Molly Smith. Forty years ago the Smiths began their woodland rhododendron garden on a five-acre parcel of land sur-

rounding their rural home. It started as most gardens do, as a hobby. At that time, Cecil farmed the flat fields that stretch to the Willamette River below their property. He grew grass for grass seed—Oregon is one of the leading suppliers to the country. Even now much of the land is still devoted to that crop.

The Smiths had no professional help in creating a grand design and merely turned to the work at hand, developing about two acres into plantings and leaving some three acres in woodland.

Although the Pacific Northwest as a whole is a great place to garden—the Japan Current does for that area what the Gulf Stream does for Great Britain—the Smiths' location is

Left, a white flowering cherry blooms behind pink *Rhododendron searsiae,* the deep pink Cecil Smith hybrid 'Relaxation', and red 'Elizabeth'. *Above,* light pink 'Exbury Naomi', yellow 'Crest', and deeper pink 'Mrs. Furnival'.

Rhododendron yakushimanum 'Ken Janeck' shares a shady spot with blue-flowered scillas and violets planted as a groundcover (foreground).

special. On a north-facing slope that is near the river, cold air drains readily off the garden. A high canopy of native trees, mainly Douglas firs, provides shelter for many of the marginally hardy plants, and the woodland acreage to the east provides an additional windbreak. The lofty and beautiful Cascade Mountains catch the warm air from the Current and in turn cause rain to fall across that area to the west of the mountains, so the garden has much the quality of a temperate rain forest—in fact, it is a temperate rain forest. A large, deep yellow form of *Rhododendron Macabeanum*, found along the Manipur-Burma border and meant for Zone 8B (temperatures found in central Florida), the fragrant *R. Edgeworthii* from the Indian State of Sikkim and happy in Zone 10, plus some mixed species of the Chinese ground orchid (*Pleione* spp.), a native of the foothills of the Himalayas, all flourish here.

Rainfall amounts to some 60 inches a year, so there is no shortage of water in this garden. Occasionally there are even torrential rains that can damage native plants in the garden. The coldest temperatures of winter rarely go below 25°F, although in a bad year they can plummet to 0°F.

The ground, as in all such forests, is rich and spongy. The Smiths never burn debris, but instead turn all the garden waste to compost, eventually returning all the goodness to the soil. Forest duff, the decaying vegetable material found in American woodlands, is a favorite planting material.

Old growth stumps of Douglas firs are covered with creeping plants of all descriptions; logs

that are left to rot upon the ground are home to ferns, mosses, and rhododendrons that require perfect drainage. In many respects, the garden could be an American version of Cambodia, and visitors need only shut their eyes for a moment in order to catch an imagined glimpse of Angkor Wat through the moss-covered trees, or to hear the rustling of a jungle python on his way to his bower.

Mr. Smith claims that he does not plant for landscape effect, yet each turn of the path provides the visitor with a new and delightful view. Plants are sited to allow them the best growing conditions — in this garden form follows function — and such planning often creates floral and textural combinations of great charm.

What began as a small enterprise now contains over six hundred selected rhododendrons (both species and hybrids), azalea varieties, and other plants acquired from growers and hybridizers both in the Portland area and throughout the world. Mr. Smith took shares in some of the plant hunting explorations to China during the 1940s in order to acquire new and choice seed.

Although there are probably over eight hundred species of *Rhododendron*, with every color

Mossy tree trunks play host to native ferns and seedling rhododendrons.

represented except for the purest of blues, gardeners and breeders continue to work for new forms and Mr. Smith has been no exception. He favors crossing the compact 3-foot shrub, *R. yakushimanum*—a reasonably hardy (Zone 6) species from Japan bearing leaves that exhibit a pronounced tomentum (they are covered with dense, woolly hairs), with more colorful mates to produce a variety of attractive progeny. Since he is most selective and particular as to form and color, he has registered and named only a handful of his hybrids.

The best known is 'Noyo Brave' (*R. yakushimanum* × 'Noyo Chief'), a marvelous plant covered with dark pink buds that open to a paler pink as the flowers age, accompanied by new leaves that are a silvery gray and as soft as the ears of a bunny. As with the parents, the leaves exhibit a thick fur or indumentum, and the bush assumes the shape of a neat mound.

Other favored plants for hybridizing are *R. Bureavii*, with its rusty red, indumented leaves; *R. Aberconwayi*, bearing simple saucer-shaped flowers of white tinged with pink; and *R. lacteum* which, with its pale yellow flowers, plays a role in the search to develop a completely hardy yellow rhododendron.

In recognition of Mr. Smith's outstanding generosity with seeds, pollen, and cuttings and his helpful advice to other gardeners, in 1985 the American Rhododendron Society (ARS) presented him their highest honor, the Pioneer Award.

Mr. Smith's selection process for the garden is very rigorous. He seeks the best forms, including the finest foliage. He has often said that a plant grows in the garden for twelve months and it should have something to offer during every one of those months, not only when it's in bloom. As a result there is a subtle blending of foliage colors and textures throughout the garden. Mr. Smith chooses plants with an eye to attractive new growth, shapely buds, indumented leaves, and fall colors, as well as attractive and beautiful blossoms. He never hesitates to use an ax on a plant that doesn't meet his standards.

As you might expect, the Smiths are interested in other plants beside rhododendrons. Many varieties of native American wildflowers, including trilliums and erythroniums, thrive in the shaded woodlands, seeding themselves with vigor and popping up all over the grounds. Patches of hardy cyclamen (*Cyclamen purpurescens*, *C. coum*, and *C. repandum* all do well), primrose, and anemone provide dots of color, and small deciduous trees and shrubs including dogwoods, styrax, silver-bells (*Halesia* spp.), birch, and others accent the evergreen foliage of the rhododendrons. Here and there clematis vines tumble through the brush.

The only pests are slugs and root weevils, but the gardens are so well tended by the volunteer help organized by the ARS that they are little bother.

Today the ARS is very important to the life of the garden. In 1984, the Smiths made it possible for the Portland Chapter of the organization to acquire their garden in order to preserve and develop it for future gardeners. Although the Smiths are still active in day-to-day affairs, the garden is now managed by a committee of ten members of the ARS. They have one permanent gardener who in turn supervises five to ten volunteers. Every Monday morning they descend on the gardens to weed, prune, and deadhead.

Hybrid seed is still sent to the ARS seed exchange and pollen to the pollen exchange. There is a continual propagation program in order to provide plants for resale in an effort to provide some funds for the garden's continued existence.

It is, in fact, amazing what two people started.

ART IN THE GARDEN

NOT TOO LONG AGO the state of garden ornamentation in America brought to mind a spate of concrete gnomes bearing names like Gustav and Hans, usually grouped around a single column, the column holding a gazing sphere of the most iridescent of chemical blues. Clearly the following words of Sir George Sitwell had often fallen upon deaf ears: "Let sculpture add yet another appeal to emotion, and the pleasure stirred by beauty in a garden may rise from massive to acute. It is not only that the statues will set off the garden; we have to consider also that the garden will set off the statues, crowning them with a garland of beauty they could not have elsewhere."

Obviously Howard and Jean Vollum had spiritually—if not literally—heard the words of Sir George when they planned and planted their home and garden near Portland, Oregon. In 1953, the Vollums built a flat-roofed home on the side of a lush hillside west of the city. The property is along the old skyline Indian Trail and a 900-foot-long, natural wooded lane curves gently up the hill through a thicket of rhododendrons, native fir trees, and cedars.

They hired landscape architect Lawrence Underhill to design a garden—eventually to cover more than two of the sixteen-acre lot—with the understanding that he consider both the needs of a growing family and that family's love of art in any plan that he undertook. And as the family grew, the house and gardens changed, continually evolving, right up to the present day.

Left, an untitled bronze sculpture by Lee Kelly rises from a mound of *Viburnum davidii* with the deep pink bloom of rhododenrons present for contrast. *Above,* an untitled bronze mother and child by Frederick Littman is surrounded by a sea of pachysandra.

Assignments to Mr. Underhill have included the protection of existing trees that stood in the way of any planned expansions of either house or grounds eventually taking away the lawns and the old drains; locating and planning a new sanitation system; integrating the inside rooms and their materials with the views outside the house; creating permanent placements for sculpture; covering the existing swimming pool; installing a standard tennis court with both lighting and a viewing area; and building a patio.

"I worked with a total concept of landscape planning," said Mr. Underhill. "That meant not only cooperating with the architect, Mel Kroker, but supervising stone masons, carpenters, swimming pool people, sculptors, electricians, tree surgeons, pruners, artists, and even a crew for the tennis courts. And even today I continue to supervise monthly maintenance."

Planning of the site was not easy because there are varying degrees of slope involved. The entrance lane climbs a five to ten percent slope with the house itself situated on an eight percent slope. A separate building called the music house was needed to house the Vollums' fifty-five rank Wurlitzer organ—originally from the San Francisco Paramount Theatre—placed below an 11-foot cut in order to save a grove of fir trees.

The tennis court, for example, was to be located in a spot with several grand Doug as firs (*Pseudotsuga Menziesii*). "In order to save the trees," said Mr. Underhill, "I sliced off the right-angle corners of the court. The path to the court leads through conifers and ferns, and is guarded by an 8-foot totem from the Canadian Northwest.

"Wind and ice are problems here," he continued, "even though this is Zone 8. The existing soil is clay with about 10 inches of topsoil. Luckily the drainage is good and all the trees are healthy.

"The Vollums raised five children in this

Top, the slate patio with built-in seating and a fire pit. Dwarf Japanese holly (*Ilex crenata* 'Compacta') runs behind the seat. *Bottom,* the stepping-stone creek that connects the two ponds.

Hilda Morris's bronze *Canyon Passage* rises from the western pond and is seen in combination with oriental poppies and iris, with staghorn sumacs (*Rhus Typhina*) across the background.

house and the original demands were to integrate art, swimming, tennis, music, science, and electronics—Howard Vollum was the founder of Tektronix Inc.—in such a way that the natural landscape was not threatened. The landscape was to be elegant, simple, and not over-planted."

Among the refinements to the house are a potting room complete with custom shelving and a sink, an equipment room, two dressing rooms, and a line of hobby benches, all for family activities. At the corner of the roof drain is a bronze spout designed by Al Goldsby. During the winter, falling rains passing through generate sounds of burbling music; in summer, a pump and roof reservoir produce the needed water.

"During the first years of the house," he said, "there was an old drive-through garage area. That became a swimming pool with an insulated roof with glass, a floor with radiant heat, and an automatic sailcloth pool cover, with everything designed to save energy costs."

Because everything is built against a slope the garage roof is low enough to step onto, so its flat surface has become a self-contained garden with built-in planters that contain vegetables and herbs. From this vantage point there is a view of the patio next to the kitchen. There Arizona flagstone and no-name slate form the floor for a raised, gas-fired barbecue pit that is surrounded with a curved 14-foot redwood bench.

As you drive up to the house you pass a bronze mother and child by Frederick Littman; the sculpture is a metal island rising from a round sea of Japanese pachysandra (*Pachysandra terminalis*). Behind the duo is a planting of Mt. Fuji cherry (*Prunus serrulata* 'Shirotae') plus hostas and rhododendrons.

The driveway continues, dividing two ponds into eastern and western circles of water. A bronze sculpture by Hilda Morris, entitled *Canyon Passage*, rises from the depths of the western pond as staghorn sumacs (*Rhus typhina*) form a background and along the drive oriental poppies and iris bloom.

"The driveway passes through two hundred and fifty rhododendrons," said Mr. Underhill, "that blend into areas of native trees. When they are in bloom it is glorious. Along the way there are plantings of moss and small perennials. I wanted to eliminate the driveway look, instead making it appear to be a path. I used 1 1/2- to 3/4-inch rock as the exposed aggregate. This textured pebble look exists beside big river boulders — they weigh between one and five tons — and carried the theme of stone right up to the stone pillars at the front door. All the stone used inside the house repeats the design; the floors are of brown no-name slate. Everything is native Oregon stone."

The house overlooks the eastern pond with its edgings of Siberian iris, pachysandra, and a another sculpture of a mother and child, this one of marble by Don Wilson, backed by an ever-red Japanese maple (*Acer palmatum*) and cut-leaf sumac (*Rhus glabra* 'Laciniata'). A maidenhair tree (*Ginkgo biloba*) — only the male tree is used as the female produces seeds with the odor of rancid butter — and a grove of black bamboo (*Phyllostachys nigra*) form a natural curtain between the house and the world outside. The two ponds are joined by a "creek:" the water runs right across (or through) the driveway, channeled between large, flat stones.

Near the crossover is an 8-foot-wide, trimmed, dwarf bird's-nest spruce (*Picea abies* 'Nidiformis'). It provides a focal point in winter. Mr. Underhill, in a bold move, had the lower branches trimmed to open them up and expose the inherent design qualities.

There is very little maintenance needed in this garden. There is no lawn. The lawn area originally installed by the Vollums was eventually replaced by the two ponds and the entry lane.

"The ponds," said Mr. Underhill, "produce a mirrored effect because the cement coating that was used to cover the bottom aggregate flooring was dyed black, creating that dark, reflective surface. A submerged pump supplies the pool's waterfalls and continually recirculates the water. The soft sound of running water, the shimmering reflections of waterlilies enhanced by the low-voltage lighting all add to a beautiful night garden."

Beyond the edges of the pond are mountain ash (*Sorbus aucuparia*) and Pacific dogwoods (*Cornus nuttallii*), while along the edge are trained shore pines (*Pinus contorta*) and *Viburnum Davidii*.

"For color," he said, "the edges of the ponds are dotted with tulips ('Peach Blossom' and 'Apricot Beauty') in the spring and salvias and geraniums in the summer. Other plants used include some magnolias, mahonia, dwarf Japanese holly (*Ilex crenata* 'Compacta'), *Vinca minor* 'Bowlesii', and *Enkianthus campanulatus*.

"I feel as though it's been the work of a lifetime to design and maintain this garden. But I've never regretted it; it's been a continual delight."

Howard Vollum died in 1986. Mrs. Vollum continues to bring new sculptures to the garden, knowing that Mr. Underhill can always find another spot for whatever she finds.

AN ECLECTIC MIX IN PORTLAND

PORTLAND, OREGON (named for Portland, Maine) lies at the junction of the Willamette and Columbia Rivers. Laid out in 1845 and incorporated in 1851, the city became the supply point for both the turmoil of the California gold fields and the Alaska gold rush.

On the southwest slope of a hill that overlooks the Willamette River, Cynthia Woodyard maintains an odd-shaped garden that totals about two-thirds of an acre. Her theme when she began some fourteen years ago was to mix attractive perennials with trees and shrubs, and make the association a happy one.

Ms. Woodyard was raised on a berry farm. In fact she drove the tractor for her father and remembers well her often prickly involvements with picking boysenberries, black-berries, and strawberries. Gardening, she says, is in her blood.

The climate is Zone 9, with winter temperatures usually staying above 20°F. "We've had windstorms, rainstorms, volcanos, and drought," she said, "but the last few winters have been mild, because my lilies of the Nile (*Agapanthus* spp.) and my *Euphorbia Wulfenii* have made it without undue damage."

Her house was built in 1932 and she found a derelict garden when she moved in. The original garden was designed by people with a penchant for the literary life, who preferred an overgrown look to method and order.

"There was a little shed in the garden," said Ms. Woodyard, "and a lilac was growing out of the roof and a cottonwood tree making

Left, a brick walk bordered with *Bergenia crassifolia* (foreground), purple *Campanula muralis,* tall spikes of *Digitalis,* and *Rosa* 'Iceberg'. Pink flowers of an unidentified old rose cultivar cover the arbor.
Above, bearded irises.

its way from the side wall. Our first job was to cut down nine old fruit and nut trees to allow the sun to shine in. And frankly, I've been working ever since."

She remembers taking gardening books to bed and reading the night away. "Especially," she said, "people like Christopher Lloyd and Alan Bloom. I learned to be patient about gardening. After all, it usually takes up to ten years to see what a garden is going to become. You can't plan and plant the first year and expect to see a mature garden the next."

"And," she added, "I did have other help to start the garden. My Swedish neighbor, Marguerite Norbo, who is eighty-five, ran a little nursery and sold perennials for years. Over that time she moved a few things from her property to mine that helped to give a sense of age to my endeavors. In fact, she still participates in what we call the Three Ladies Plant Sale, that we hold every spring.

"But the children have grown up and moved out, so I'm really alone in the garden. I do try and get an occasional neighborhood child to help out with pruning but that's not always so successful either."

Her garden is an eclectic mix. There is one view of a brick path that looks to a bower of roses. In front are luxurious bergenias (*Bergenia* × *Schmidtii*), while the pathway is lined with blooming *Campanula Portenschlagiana* on either side, and on the left is a large Calamondin orange or orangequat (× *Citrofortunella mitis*) tree, that is moved into her small 8- by 5-foot greenhouse to winter over, along with many of her agapanthus.

"My brother put in the brick paving for the walkways and he and my father built a small pond, 3 feet deep and about a 5- by 6-foot rectangle. There's a pump and the sound of water splashing to entertain the four huge fish who live there. The plants are yellow water flags (*Iris pseudacorus*); I haven't gotten to waterlilies yet. I've recently discovered regular lilies: they are rare, though, gorgeous, and often fragrant, and readily stuck in empty spots in the border.

"I started out loving the English garden," she said, "but now I like a subtropical look: a touch of Italy, a dash of Hawaii, even a bit of Santa Barbara. And I love the seasons, the soil, sunshine, mulches, and even the worms of gardening. But the most magical thing are the gardeners themselves and the very private and special things about each one."

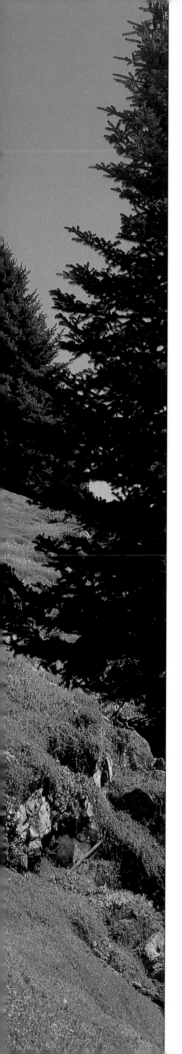

PATTERNS ON A NORTHWEST LANDSCAPE

"To make a great garden," wrote Sir George Sitwell, in his book, *On the Making of Gardens*, "one must have a great idea or a great opportunity; a cypress causeway leading to a giant's castle, or a fountain cave where a ceaseless iris* plays on a river falling through the roof, or a deep clear pool with an underworld fantasy of dragon-guarded treasure caves lit by unearthly light . . . or a precipitous ravine with double bridges and a terrace on either hand."

Sir Sitwell wrote the above in 1909 so it's obvious he never saw the Ohme gardens, but from the description above, he could have visited them in his mind's eye. Herman Ohme, the founder of the gardens, was graced with both of Sitwell's requirements: a great idea when he decided to plant his arid slopes with thousands of evergreens and low-growing alpine plants, and a great opportunity in a site that overlooks an open and beautiful valley divided by the Columbia River and in the distance, the Cascade Mountains.

Wenatchee, Washington, is near the confluence of the Columbia and Wenatchee rivers. In 1929, Herman Ohme and his bride, Ruth, bought forty acres of land located about three miles north of the city to establish a fruit orchard. Mr. Ohme had been born in the flatlands of Illinois and throughout his youth he had yearned for the rugged mountains of the West.

When the Ohmes began their garden the location was dry and desolate. Scatterings of desert sage (*Artemisia tripartita*) and grease-

*An iris in this use is a kind of rock crystal that reflects prismatic colors.

Left, sedums carpet a hillside. *Above,* a stone bench from which to view the gardens.

A stone path winds
among sedums
planted as
groundcovers.

wood (*Sarcobatus vermiculatus*) covered outcrops — a welcome addition to the bare rock, but not enough to really raise the spirit.

"They began in a small way," said Gordon Ohme, the youngest of two sons and now in charge of the operation that pilots the garden. "In an old Studebaker coupe, my mother and father would drive up to their property from the family house at the base of the hill, with the rumble seat packed to overflowing with small evergreens, chiefly Douglas fir (*Pseudotsuga Menzeissii*) and western yellow pine (*Pinus ponderosa*). They planted the trees in between the outcroppings and carried the water up from the valley below. They hauled native stone to form pathways and trails and borders for the various beds. Using nothing except his back, my father either rolled rocks into place or he used a crowbar. Why they even used a mule and a drag bucket to carve out the first pool."

The outlines of the various trails that wind about the garden and the steps are constructed of a chunky type of rock taken right from the hill. The basic rockwork is then paved with flagstone that the Ohmes worked into slabs with the time-honored method of a sledge hammer and a wedge. Today the rock is hauled in by a truck but still carried to the final site by hand.

"It would be easier," Mr. Ohme said, "to use concrete or asphalt as a surface for the paths but that's unthinkable in a natural site such as this."

The original plan was to create a small retreat, a quiet place to walk to at the end of a busy day in the orchards, but like many things, the garden soon took on a life of its own and began to grow.

After the first ten years the developing gardens covered several acres and the spot of green on the otherwise barren hill began to attract attention from the valley below. Visitors to the gardens

Top, a quiet stream trickles down a slope planted with sedums. *Bottom,* stone walkways criss-cross the side of a hill. A slope planted with sedums and Douglas firs.

suggested that it be opened to the public, which officially came to pass in 1939.

As the gardens grew, the problems of maintenance also increased and luckily Gordon Ohme showed a pronounced interest in and ability to work the land. By the time he had graduated from high school he had become as dedicated to the garden as his parents. He has now logged over thirty-six years in the family pursuit.

"My parents did little," he said, "to publicize their work but word soon spread and by the 1950s the annual number of visitors was nearing 20,000 and the gardens that now covered five acres were gradually becoming self-supporting. The grounds are open from April to October and all our time is devoted to weeding, watering, trimming, deadheading, cutting lawns, and the general type of cleanup that is a constant part of operating an endeavor like this. But the work is never over because during the late fall and winter we spend time developing new areas as the gardens continue to grow. Last year we had over 35,000 visitors."

In order to plant the newly developed areas, small plugs of the various groundcovers are taken from the older established areas much like plugs for a hair transplant operation. The plugs are set a foot or so apart and after three to four years they grow together to completely cover the ground.

Although winters in Washington are generally not considered brutal (winter temperatures rarely go below 0°F.) they do arrive with a lot of rain or snow, so there is no problem with water. But for five or six months during the summer there is a pronounced drop in the rainfall, yet the gardens need water not only for irrigating the plants but also for the waterfalls, streams, and pools that are part of the grand design.

During the garden's youth, the Ohmes had to dig trenches to bury pipelines to carry water up from the valley below, and watering

Opposite, stately
Douglas firs
provide a rich
green backdrop for
a hillside softly
washed with the
color of sedums.

was accomplished with hoses and sprinklers. But in the 1960s, Gordon Ohme installed an intricate and practically invisible system of sprinklers set among the rock formations. Only the top of the sprinkler head is visible and even with over one hundred and twenty five of them installed, most visitors never notice their presence and the goal of a natural looking garden is preserved.

"On an average summer night," Mr. Ohme said, "we use over 130,000 gallons of water."

The stones, the trees, plants, and the pools are so skillfully blended with the existing rock formations that all look as though they've been in place for eons. The evergreens and low-growing plants have created both a rain forest and an alpine meadow. The fern-shaded pools, for example, resemble those left behind when the glaciers retreated one hundred centuries ago. And during the spring, from a distance the gardens are transformed into the pastoral retreat of a benevolent race of giants who have applied broad strokes of color with a brush dipped in petals.

The gardens are most colorful in the months from April to mid-June. Using creeping phlox (*Phlox stolonifera*), many kinds of creeping thyme (*Thymus* spp.), dianthus (*Dianthus deltoides*), several varieties of sedum, including dragon's blood sedum (*Sedum spurium* 'Dragon's Blood') and myrtle (*Vinca minor*), the colors carpet the land like a patchwork quilt. The stitching is provided by Irish moss (*Soleirolia Soleirolii*) in use along the rocks of the pathways.

Basket-of-gold (*Aurinia saxatilis*) and blue ajuga (*Ajuga reptans*) creep over the edges of the steps. Native ferns, chiefly maidenhair (*Adiantum pedatum*) and maidenhair spleenwort (*Asplenium Trichomanes*) plus wildflowers including trilliums (*Trillium* spp.), border one beautiful pool that is more like a setting for a German opera than a garden in the mountains.

"But the garden is basically green," said Mr. Ohme, "for a good share of the year. The colors are only there in the spring. Over the years we've transplanted over a thousand evergreen trees from the Cascade Mountains. We start when trees are about the size of a broomstick and some now have diameters of over 3 feet. Although my father began with the western yellow pine we've eliminated them because of the size they became over the years. We still use western red cedar (*Thuja plicata*) and grand fir (*Abies grandis*) from the wetter and higher areas, but most of the trees we transplant today are mountain hemlocks (*Tsuga Mertensiana*) and alpine firs (*Abies lasiocarpa*) from the high country. They all succeed in this one location."

In 1971 Herman Ohme died at the age of eighty, but his wife, Ruth, still helps out with the gardens and with meeting the public. "Either my wife, Carol, my mother, or I," said Mr. Ohme, "are at the entrance to the gardens from opening to closing. People come in bus tours or carloads at a time and sometimes over weekends the parking lot can get to be pretty full. But anyone who comes in talks to an Ohme. I have a niece and a daughter-in-law who also help and my son just passed me on his way to do an errand."

Mr. Ohme's favorite gardening quote was found in a copy of the *Reader's Digest*. It appears on the brochure that describes his family's garden to visitors and strangely enough, it was penned by Sir Osbert Sitwell, son of Sir George: "Green is the clue to creating a garden, not the possession of all the hues in the rainbow. The most beautiful gardens in the world show few flowers. They depend for their beauty on trees, stone, and water, and on the prospect which their terraces frame. These gardens are created for rest in cool surroundings, for idleness and sauntering and imaginative thought, for love and a sense of mystery."

PART TWO

Great Ideas for Your Garden

INTRODUCTION

It's one thing to look over page after page of glorious garden photos, being kept in a state of perpetual envy by the passing parade of spectacular flowers (and requisite settings), and quite another to achieve the same effect in your own backyard, especially if you are short of time or help or both.

But it can be done. Many of the gardens that we have just toured were planned and executed by individuals who learned how to employ active imaginations and boundless enthusiasm in an effort to strike a balance between marvelous effects and the outlay of a reasonable amount of effort.

Most of those gardeners read garden books whenever possible in order to continually assimilate the ideas of others. Most of them are willing to expend the sheer amount of energy needed to develop and maintain a showplace garden; most of them have raised their own plants from seed or cuttings in order to expand their collections beyond the ordinary; and most of them have experimented with plants and taken chances

both with their particular climates and their individual locations. They have looked for and found solutions using a creative approach rather then slavishly copying the most commonplace approaches.

If a rock needed to be moved in order to complete a garden picture and the rock could not be moved, the gardeners thought of and tried other solutions to the problem. If a garden was on a precipitous slope, the gardeners built their own terracing. If water was in short supply, plants were brought in that could withstand prolonged drought. In fact, there is hardly an obstacle placed in a true gardener's path that the gardener cannot find a way around.

This section of the book is meant to inspire your own creativity. These pages contain some ideas that can be adapted to fit a variety of garden situations. First, there are pictures of gardens in winter, early spring, late spring, and fall, not only summer.

There are also examples of gardening in containers. Container gardening is a great way to change your garden's look and to feature plants that might be unhappy if you left them outdoors all year in your climate. Containers also give you a place for color if you only have a terrace or patio for gardening.

Pictures of garden ornaments highlight the important part that man-made objects—or those found either in nature or even at a garage sale—can play in the design of the garden.

Various examples of paths illustrate the necessity of a way to get around and through flower beds and plantings, and the different ways that this can be accomplished.

Finally, this section includes pictures of some unusual plants to try in your own garden, plants that are available from the nurseries listed in the Appendix, either as mature specimens or seeds.

Making a Plan

I have been gardening for over twenty years at my own volition and many more seasons, as a child, under the watchful eye of parents who wanted help in maintaining the backyard. Over those years I have often felt that my successes could be listed on the pages of a small notebook while my failures would fill volumes! This last is the inevitable feeling that most gardeners are confronted with as a result of working directly with living things and not just a philosophy of life. Even then it is possible to learn an amazing number of lessons from those failures.

There are a great number of plants that I have recorded over the years that have simply refused to grow in my garden regardless of the care that I have lavished upon them. There are many more that have survived a few of our winters—usually in marginal condition—only to eventually give up the ghost and pass away. I've mulched and dug and dug and mulched but there is one thing that I find myself continually guilty of: I forget to plan out my garden movements in advance.

Like many of the gardeners in this book, my heart is larger than my head, and every spring I order a great number of plants and there is simply no place to put them. If I would stop and make a simple plan of the garden, I would know where to put them rather than wandering around with a helpless look on my face.

If I could give you any word of advice it would be this: Before you start any garden—whether it is your own design or based on ideas in this book (or others like it)—take a pencil and paper and sketch a simple layout of the area to be developed.

The map need not be an art object, but such a plan will save you time, energy, money, and often much grief. It need not have complicated contour lines and surveyor's symbols. In short, just a quick sketch will do.

Only you can decide how much land you wish to take care of and how much time you will have free for garden chores. Remember that all gardens require a certain amount of care. They need weeding, mulching, cultivating, clipping, and all the pick-up work that goes along with garden activities.

Consider, too, that all gardening takes more time than you expect it will (usually because it's so pleasant an activity that you forget the passing of the hours). Very few things can look more dismal to you—and your neighbors—than an abandoned site with a few worn-out plants surrounded by weeds. By working out a simple plan you will be able to concentrate your thoughts and organize your activities.

Seasonal Specialties

*A*ny garden with living plants is in a continual state of change as young plants mature and older plants reach and pass their prime. But gardens are always at their best when they contain enough plant variety that all the seasons of the year have their own special highlights. The following photographs demonstrate that while spring is always a burst of color and summer a time of exuberance, fall can be aglow with tempered shades and even winter can be especially beautiful under a shallow carpet of snow.

The garden in winter presents a more peaceful aspect than at any other season in the year. Here a once sparkling but now stilled fountain becomes a serene sculpture as snow blankets the trees and ground.

Harry Lauder's walking stick (*Corylus Avellana* 'Contorta') becomes a focal point in a winter garden, its tortured branches twisting against the snow. Male flowers in drooping catkins appear before the leaves in late winter or early spring.

One of the first flowers of the new year is the winter aconite (*Eranthis hyemalis*), with buttercup-like flowers that bloom as the snow melts around them. It is perfect for planting in drifts but requires excellent drainage.

Above, the unbounding enthusiasm of late spring is typified by a clematis vine (*Clematis montana*) growing at Western Hills nursery, as it seems to swallow everything in its path with glorious flowers. *Opposite page top,* a mid-spring gathering of triumph tulips (*Tulipa* 'Golden Melody') mixed in with a planting of old-fashioned ribbon grass or gardener's garters (*Phalaris arundinacea* var. *picta*). *Opposite page bottom,* the red flowers are a long-lasting wild tulip from Iran (*Tulipa Eichleri*) with intensely scarlet petals and a yellow-margined center. They last for years in a perennial bed.

A gazebo surrounded by the mellow glow of autumn is a perfect place to contemplate the past glories of the summer.

In the author's garden, ornamental grasses welcome the shortened days of fall. Clockwise from the top are Chinese silver grass (*Miscanthus floridulus*), Ravenna grass (*Erianthus ravennae*), cord grass (*Spartina pectinata* 'Aureomarginata'), and eulalia grass (*M. sinensis*).

The rockspray cotoneaster (*Cotoneaster horizontalis*) is a hardy shrub that will spread over rocks just like a waterfall. It bears bright red berries in fall and winter.

Gardens in Containers

*T*he great thing about gardening in containers is the ability to move them about the landscape in order to create new combinations that always glorify the plant and often the pot. Short-lived bulbs can be enjoyed for the moment then stored away and a new flower can take the stage. Even tropical plants can be wintered indoors yet find a summer home on the patio or in the perennial border of a northern garden. Remember to provide adequate drainage for plants in containers and be careful to keep up the watering schedule, especially during hot weather. Always check for insect pests before bringing plants back indoors for the winter.

Opposite, three pots add more color to a summer garden, sitting on the edge of a rock wall. From the left are *Sequoia sempervirens* 'Adpressa', *Kochia* 'Acapulco Silver', and an ornamental grass (*Koeleria glauca*).

Left, half of a wine barrel makes a perfect home for fancy-leafed caladiums (*Caladium × hortulanum*) in mixed varieties and some impatiens (*Impatiens* spp.) for added color.

Below, a beautiful glazed pot holds an ancient member of the cycad family in company with a bevy of blooming terrestrial orchids (*Pleione formosana*).

Above, some hen-and-chicken hybrids (*Sempervivum* spp.) and rock lichen have grown from seed (and spore) deposited in the crevice of a large rock and the rock has become a very large container.

Opposite, late in the year, a Hollywood juniper (*Juniperus chinensis* 'Kaizuka') adds the green to an autumn garden. Because it would suffer in below-zero winds, the conifer spends the winter in an unheated sunporch.

Left, some unknown wild grasses have been transplanted into a decorative urn and four simpler pots to make a stunning addition to the edge of a terrace. *Opposite,* a wrought-iron planter is home to pots of brilliant red geraniums that bloom in a South Carolina garden.

A fourteen-year-old cabbage palm (*Cordyline australis*) is brought out in a large pot to bring a touch of tropical drama to my garden in Zone 5. The plant spends the winter in a cold greenhouse.

In this garden brightly colored pots are in direct contrast to a variety of colorful annuals, demonstrating that containers need not always be in neutral shades of white or brown.

Statuary and Ornaments

Just as a room for living requires furniture and ornaments, so does a garden. Once the concrete and painted gnome ruled supreme in America's backyards, but today a gardener can find Japanese lanterns, brass sundials, stone casts of Roman faces, found objects of every description, and copies of garden sculpture from the world's great museums. Furniture makers now produce benches that will last for decades. Even outdoor lights are available that can easily be installed by anyone who can hold a shovel, turn a screwdriver, and spare a few hours of time.

A bed of summer perennials is watched over by a cast concrete diva of the garden.

A fanciful snail is caught throwing water to the winds over the surface of an ornamental pond. This clever fountain brings an element of whimsy to the garden in addition to the sweet sounds of falling water on a hot summer's afternoon.

Amid the bountiful bloom of western daisies, a bleached cow skull taken from an Arizona desert becomes a natural sculpture, its stark organic form in direct contrast to the dainty flower petals.

Opposite, a pottery figure peers out from a mass of summer foliage as it keeps its eye on the garden.

Right, a lead elephant in the Hester garden seems impervious to the winter's cold and ready for a walk around the garden.

Below, an empty pottery jug and a saucer that becomes a reflecting pool, add drama to the Huyghes' summer garden.

A glazed jar picks up the soft lavender color of sprays of Russian sage (*Perovskia atriplicifolia*).

A cast concrete foo dog gazes out from the fall foliage and berries of a rockspray cotoneaster (*Cotoneaster horizontalis*).

A stone reflecting pool and some Pacific Coast hybrid irises.

An armillary-type sundial stands in front of zebra grass (*Miscanthus sinensis* 'Zebrinus') and a mass of Symons-Jeune phlox (*Phlox* 'White Admiral'). The lilies (*Lilium formosanum*) in the foreground bloom in September.

Paths and Paving

No matter how beautiful the garden, there must be a way to get from one part of it to another without continually disturbing the plants. And just as the yellow brick road led Dorothy and her friends to Oz, so a pathway becomes a beckoning invitation to explore the garden. Even the smallest of gardens can benefit from a wandering and curving thoroughfare that leads off either to the left or the right, promising more beauty around the next bend. Flagstones, flat rocks, boulders, bricks, gravel, concrete slabs, and even turf can be used to great effect. The cracks between stones or slabs can be seeded with creeping plants like the thymes and the camomiles.

Opposite, an edging of large stones and paths of grass are perfect for the informal look of this wildflower garden in New England. *Right,* a pathway made of timbers cut on edge and silvered by exposure to wind and weather makes a happy contrast to the sun-loving plants that grow next to it.

Terracing made
from a river of
rocks that snakes
its way down a
California hillside in
the Eliels' garden.

A walkway of weathered brick divides a beautiful bed of annual flowers including petunias, cosmos, and gloriosa daisies.

A flagstone walk through turf leads to steps and then a small terrace that in summer becomes the home for many potted plants.

A country garden is divided by a grassy path lined on either side with common bricks set in a few inches of sand.

A stream of *Echeveria* meanders past a bank of *Aloe striata* hybrids in Harland Hand's garden.

SOURCES OF SUPPLY

———

BIBLIOGRAPHY

SOURCES OF SUPPLY

Plant Societies.

There are well over one hundred plant societies in the United States and Canada. All of them publish excellent newsletters or bulletins. Many sponsor seed exchanges or act as clearing houses for the exchange of cuttings. The following are only a sample.

American Conifer Society, 1825 North 72 Street, Philadelphia, PA 19151.

American Horticultural Society, Mount Vernon, VA 22121.

American Hemerocallis Society, Route 5, Box 874, Palatka, FL 32077.

American Hosta Society, 9448 Mayfield Road, Chesterland OH 44026.

American Penstemon Society, Box 33, Plymouth, VT 05056.

American Primrose Society, 6730 West Mercer Way, Mercer Island, WA 98040.

American Rhododendron Society, 14635 S.W. Bull Mountain Road, Tigrad, OR 97223.

American Rock Garden Society, c/o Buffy Parker, 15 Fairmead Road, Darien, CT 06820.

American Rose Society, Box 30,000, Shreveport, LA 71130.

Cactus and Succulent Society of America, 2631 Fairgreen Ave., Arcadia, CA 91006.

Herb Society of America, 300 Massachusetts Ave, Boston, MA 02115.

Heritage Rose Group, Patricia Cole, Drawer K, Mesilla, NM 88046.

Perennial Plant Association, 217 Howlett Hall, 2001 Fyffe Court, Columbus, OH 43210.

Waterlily Society of America, Box 104, Lilypons, MD 21717.

The Directory of Regional Gardening Resources is compiled by the Horticultural Committee of The Garden Club of America. It divides the United States into seven regions and offers for each region: (1) publications dealing with that area; (2) nurseries emphasizing those that propagate their own plant material; and (3) demonstration gardens and arboreta where gardeners may see the particular plants from their areas. The book is available from Garden Club of America, 598 Madison Avenue, New York, NY 10022. The cost is $5.50 including postage.

Commercial Seed Companies

The Country Garden, Route 2, Crivitz, WI 54114. Annuals and perennials.

Far North Garden, 16785 Harrison, Livonia MI 48154. Primroses and wildflowers.

The Fragrant Path, Box 328, Fort Calhoun, NE 68023. Fragrant plants and flowers.

J. L. Hudson, Seedsman, P. O. Box 1058, Redwood City, CA 94064. Many seeds from around the world.

Maver Rare Perennials, Route 2, Box 265B, Asheville, NC 28805. Wide range of seeds including ornamental grasses.

Geo. W. Park Seed Company, Greenwood, SC 29647. One of the largest seed companies with many unusual plants.

Plants of the Southwest, 1812 Second Street, Sante Fe, NM 87501. Wildflowers and grasses from the Southwest.

Prairie Nursery, P. O. Box 365, Westfield, WI 53964. Wildflowers and ornamental grasses from the prairies.

Clyde Robin Seed Company, P. O. Box 2855, Castro Valley, CA 94546. Major dealer in wildflower seeds.

Seeds Blüm, Idaho City Stage, Boise, ID 83706. Heirloom seeds.

Stock Seed Farms, Inc., R.R. #1, Box 112, Murdock, NE 68407. Wildflowers and prairie grasses.

Thompson and Morgan, Box 1308, Jackson, NJ 08527. Huge catalog of seeds.

Mail-Order Nurseries

Alpenglow, 13328 King George Highway, Surrey, B.C., Canada V3T 2T6. Alpines, perennials, and shrubs.

Appalachian Gardens, Box 82, Waynesboro, PA 17268. Unusual perennials and shrubs.

Bernardo Beach Native Plant Farm, Star Route 7, Box 145, Vesquita, NM 87062. Perennials, vines, shrubs, wildflowers, and cacti for southwestern gardens.

Kurt Bluemel, Inc., 2543 Hess Road, Fallston, MD 21047. World's largest nursery in ornamental grasses.

B & D Lilies, 330 P Street, Port Townsend, WA 98368. All kinds of lilies for the garden.

Busse Gardens, Route 2, Box 238, Cokato, MN 55321. All-around selection of perennials.

The Bovees Nursery, 1737 S. W. Coronado, Portland, OR 97219. Rhododendrons, azaleas, and companion plants.

The Cummings Garden, 22 Robertsville Road, Marlboro, NJ. 07746. Dwarf and small evergreens and companion plants.

Daystar, RFD 2, Litchfield, ME 04350. Dwarf conifers and small shrubs.

Donaroma's Nursery, Box 2189, Edgartown, MA 02539. Wildflowers and perennials.

Endangered Species, Box 1830, Tustin, CA 92681. Bamboos, grasses, and unusual plants.

Fjellgarden, P.O. Box 1111, Lakeside, AZ 85929. Unusual alpine plants.

Garden Place, 6780 Heisley Road, P. O. Box 83, Mentor, OH 44060. All-around selection of perennials.

Girard Nurseries, P.O. Box 428, Geneva, Ohio 44041. Small evergreens and hollies.

Glasshouse Works, Church St., Box 97, Stewart, OH 45778. Tropicals and many unusual plants.

Greer Gardens, 1280 Goodpasture Road, Eugene, OR 97401. Rhododendrons, azaleas, and companion plants.

High Country Rosarium, 1717 Downing Street, Denver, CO 80218. Large selecion of roses.

Holbrook Farm, Route 2, Box 223B, Fletcher, NC 28732. Wide range of perennials.

Klehm & Son, Route 5, Box 197, South Barrington, IL 60010. Peonies, daylilies, hostas, and iris.

Lamb's Nurseries, E. 101 Sharp Avenue, Spokane, WA 99202. Perennials, alpines, and garden mums.

Las Pilitas Nursery, Star Route, Box 23x, Santa Margarita, CA 93453. Native California plants.

Logee's Greenhouses, Danielson, CT 06239. Tropicals and many herbs.

Lowe's Own Root Roses, 6 Sheffield Road, Nashua, NH 03062. New and rare roses.

J. D. Lyon, 143 Alewife Brook Parkway, Cambridge, MA 02140. Select collection of bulbs.

McClure & Zimmerman, 108 W. Winnebago, P. O. Box 368, Friesland, WI 53935. Large collection of bulbs.

Milaeger's Gardens, 4838 Douglas Avenue, Racine, WI 53402. Large collection of perennials.

Putney Nursery, Inc., Putney, VT 05346. American wildflowers.

Rice Creek Gardens, 1315 66th Avenue Northeast, Minneapolis, MN 55432. Rock garden plants and alpines.

Rocknoll Nursery, 9210 U.S. 50, Hillsboro, OH 45133. Rock garden plants and hardy perennials.

Roses of Yesterday and Today, Brown's Valley Road, Watsonville, CA 95076. Old fashioned roses.

Sandy Mush Herbs, Route 2, Surrett Cove Road, Leicester, NC 28748. Diverse collection of herbs and perennials.

Siskiyou Rare Plant Nursery, 2825 Cummings Road, Medford, OR 97501. Rare alpines and rock garden plants.

Shady Oaks Nursery, 700 19th Avenue N.E., Waseca, MN 66093. Large collection of plants for shady places.

John Scheepers, Inc., Philipsburg Road, R.D. 2, Middletown, NY 10940. Many bulbs including lilies.

Louis Smirnow, 85 Linden Lane, Glen Head, Brookville, NY 11545. Tree peonies and herbaceous peonies.

Stallings Nursery, 910 Encenitas Boulevard, Encenitas, CA 92024. Unusual collection of tropicals and grasses.

Surry Gardens, P.O. Box 145, Surry, ME 04684. Large selection of perennials.

Andre Viette Farm & Nursery, Route 1, Box 16, Fishersville, VA 22939. Daylilies, hostas, and ornamental grasses.

Wayside Gardens, Hodges, SC 29695. Perennials and shrubs. WeDu Nursery, Route 5, Box 724, Marion, NC 28752. Large collection of native wildflowers.

White Flower Farm, Litchfield, CT 06759. Large number of perennials.

Gilbert H. Wild, Sarcoxie, MO 64862. Peonies and daylilies.

Woodlanders, 1128 Colleton Avenue, Aiken, SC 29801. Wildflowers, native shrubs, and trees.

The following books are a few of the many written about gardening in America. It is purely a personal selection based on the books I have found most useful for working in my garden. Few of them will be found in today's bookstores. Most, if not all, can be found by visiting your local library or searching the catalogs of second hand book dealers.

Barr, Claude A. *Jewels of the Plains*. Minneapolis: University of Minnesota Press, 1983. American wildflower lore and instruction written by a South Dakota rancher.

Blanchan, Neltje. *The American Flower Garden*. New York: Doubleday, Page & Company, 1909. A marvelous book about planning and growing an American garden.

———— *Nature's Garden*. New York: Doubleday, Page & Co., 1904. One of the two best books on American wildflowers ever written.

Britton, Nathaniel Lord, and Addison Brown. *An Illustrated Flora of the Northern United States and Canada*. 3 vols. 1913. Reprint. New York: Dover, 1970. Covers most of the wild plants growing in the U. S.

Dana, Mrs. William Starr. *How to Know the Wild Flowers*. New York: Charles Scribner's Sons, 1895. The other best book on American wildflowers.

Earle, Alice Morse. *Old Time Gardens*. New York: The Macmillan Company, 1901. Readable and delightful history of American gardens.

Ferber, Linda S., and William H. Gerdts. *The New Path: Ruskin and the American Pre-Raphaelites*. Brooklyn: The Brooklyn Museum, 1985. Flower art created in a little-known American art movement.

Free, Montague. *All About the Perennial Garden*. New York: Doubleday & Company, 1955. A book on starting a garden by a former horticulturist of the Brooklyn Botanic Garden.

Foster, H. Lincoln, and Laura Louise Foster. *Rock Gardens*. Portland, Oregon: Timber Press, 1982. The original American book on rock gardening and still one of the best.

From Seed to Flower: Philadelphia 1681-1876. Philadelphia: The Pennsylvania Horticultural Society, 1976. A history of gardening in America.

Hortus Third. New York: Macmillan, 1976. The major work on botanical nomenclature for America.

Jensen, Jens. *Siftings*. Chicago: Ralph Fletcher Seymour, 1939. Horticultural writings by a forgotten American genius.

Lay, Charles Downing. *A Garden Book for Autumn and Winter*. New York: Duffield & Company, 1924. Trees, shrubs, and plants for two neglected seasons of the year.

Leighton, Ann. *American Gardens in the Eighteenth Century*. Boston: Houghton Mifflin Company, 1976. Many histories of American gardens.

Loewer, H. Peter. *Growing and Decorating with Grasses*. New York: Walker and Company, 1977. One of two American books on ornamental grasses.

McCully, Anderson. *American Alpines in the Garden*. New York: The Macmillan Company, 1931. A rock garden book that deals exclusively with American wildflowers.

Meyer, Mary Hockenberry. *Ornamental Grasses*. New York: Charles Scribner's Sons, 1975. The other book on ornamental grasses in America.

Miller, Everitt L., and Jay S. Miller. *The American Garden Guidebook*. New York: M. Evans and Company, Inc., 1987. A new guidebook to American gardens with 339 listings.

Miles, Bebe. *Wildflower Perennials for Your Garden*. New York: Hawthorn, 1976. Garden plans and plant lore on American wildflowers.

Nuese, Josephine. *The Country Garden*. New York: Charles Scribner's Sons, 1970. The thirty-five year story of an American garden.

Ortloff, Henry Stuart. *A Garden Bluebook of Annuals and Biennials*. New York: Doubleday, Doran & Company, Inc., 1931. An old and treasured book about annuals.

Smith, J. Robert, with Beatrice S. Smith. *The Prairie Garden*. Madison, Wisconsin: The University of Wisconsin Press, 1980. Landscaping with and growing native American plants.

Taylor, Norman, editor. *The Practical Encyclopedia of Gardening*. New York: Garden City Publishing Company, Inc., 1936. Look for this edition. It is the best.

Thomas, Jr. George C. *The Practical Book of Outdoor Rose Growing*. Philadelphia: J. B. Lippincott Company, 1917. An excellent guide on growing roses in America.

Wilder, Louise Beebe. *Adventures in My Garden and Rock Garden*. New York: Doubleday, Page & Company, 1923.

———— *Hardy Bulbs*. New York: Dover Publications, Inc., 1974. Delightful and readable books about American gardening.

Wilson, E. H. *America's Greatest Garden*. Boston: The Stratford Company, 1925. The story of the Arnold Arboretum.

Wright, Richardson. *The Practical Book of Outdoor Flowers*. Philadelphia: J. B. Lippincott Company, 1924. An excellent book of advice for starting a garden.

Wyman, Donald. *Shrubs & Vines for American Gardens*. New York: Macmillan Publishing Co., Inc., 1977.

———— *Wyman's Gardening Encyclopedia*. New York: The Macmillan Company, 1971. Two invaluable books on gardening in America.

INDEX

Italic page numbers denote illustrations

PHOTOGRAPHY CREDITS

Judith Bromley, pp. 86–89. Ken Druse, pp. 36–45, 124–127, 169. Alan Eliel, pp. 106–107, 109 (bottom), 111, 180. Derek Fell, pp. 46–49, 56–59, 112–117, 128–131, 148–153, 158, 159 (bottom), 161–162, 164 (bottom), 171–172, 173 (top), 174 (top) 178, 181 (top). Felice Frankel, pp. 102–105. Robert Frasier, p. 96. Pamela J. Harper, pp. 2–5, 30–34, 64–68, 118–122, 174 (bottom), 176 (top), 183. Margaret A. Hensel, pp. 16–19, 20–23. Bruce Krasberg, pp. 80–85. Peter Loewer, pp. 50–55, 159 (top), 160, 163, 164 (top), 165–167, 170, 175, 176 (bottom), 177 (bottom), 182, 184–188. Beth Maynor, pp. 70–73. Elvin McDonald, p. 168. Gary Mottau, pp. 6–15, 24–28, 181 (bottom). John Neubauer, p. 60. John Occelli, pp. 98, 100, 101 (top). Doan Ogden, pp. 74–79. Joanne and Jerry Pavia, title page, pp. 132–136, 144–147. Kathlene Persoff, p. 177 (top). Judith Phillips, pp. 173 (bottom), 179, 184–185, 189. Larry Rhodes, pp. 108, 109 (top), 110. Allan R. Taylor, pp. 90–95. Tom Tynan, pp. 97, 101 (bottom). Volkmar K. Wentzel, pp. 61–63.